PURE
FOOD

PURE FOOD

How to

SHOP, COOK AND HAVE FUN IN YOUR KITCHEN **EVERY DAY.**

Christine Cushing

PHOTOGRAPHY BY
Bill Milne

whitecap

Edited by Nicole de Montbrun
Proofread by Marilyn Bittman
Design by Patricia Papadakos
Cover photography and introduction page by Tim Leyes
Printed in Canada by Friesens

Library and Archives Canada Cataloguing in Publication
Cushing, Christine

Pure food: how to shop, cook and have fun in your kitchen every day/
Christine Cushing.

Includes index.
ISBN 978-1-55285-901-8
ISBN 1-55285-901-0

1. Cookery. I. Title.
TX714.C88 2007   641.5   C2007-901701-0

The publisher acknowledges the financial support of the Government of Canada
through the Book Publishing Industry Development Program (BPIDP) and the
province of British Columbia through the Book Publishing Tax Credit.

FOR MY FATHER

What is the secret of Christine Cushing's success? Whether she's cooking on television or at home, working in a restaurant kitchen or putting together some glamorous gala for a worthy cause, she has a style that is satisfyingly her own. She has an instinct for finding the point of balance between the sensual and the sensible. Between the practical and the inspired. Between dishes you cook for candlelit dinner parties and dishes for every day. And, more than anything else, her food tastes wonderful.

This book is full of recipes for real people with real lives to lead. They don't take forever to cook or require a team of assistants. They do acknowledge the importance of seasonality and nutrition but they temper that righteousness with a delightfully easygoing and cosmopolitan approach. "Cooking should always be fun," she says. That's right up there with flavor in Christine's kitchen.

And practical wisdom…now that we care so much about where our ingredients come from, Christine's advice on shopping and how to stock our pantries and refrigerators is particularly timely. Her cooking is ingredient-driven — which may have something to do with her Greek heritage. Her attitude to shopping certainly reminds me of the way Greek women go about it in the small towns of the Ionian and Aegean islands. For them, shopping is a conversational activity, built on longstanding relationships with the butcher, the greengrocer, the baker, and the fishmonger. With trust and that kind of rapport, the chore becomes a source of pleasure and inspiration. And the quality of what you eat soars.

Pure Food is a book that is guaranteed to be free of all artificial additives, including pretentiousness. Smart, practical, fun and, above all, delicious, *Pure Food* is pure Christine Cushing.

—James Chatto

I'D LIKE TO THANK THE FOLLOWING PEOPLE

FOR HELPING ME GET THIS BOOK

OFF THE GROUND:

Bosko — for your undying enthusiasm, love, and support. *Robert McCullough* at Whitecap Books — for acquiring the project and making every meeting a blast. *Bill Milne and his team* — for showcasing your many talents and hosting us at your New York studio to take the photos. *Matt Kimura* — for coming into the jungle with me to test and retest the recipes. *My mom Georgia* — for always lending a hand and a huge thanks and a hug for helping with all the prep work and doing the dishes for the recipe development process. *Gus* at City Fish Market in Toronto — for providing me with the most beautiful seafood for these recipes. I highly recommend a trip to see Gus. *Nicole, my editor* — for keeping things on track when my Greek mind wanted to wander. *Lianne* — for braving the 5 am ice storm and coming out to do such a great job on my hair and makeup for the photo shoot. *Trish Papadakos* — for capturing the essence of my book with your fresh and dynamic sense of design. You are truly talented.

It's a fact: we eat every day. We go to work, pick up the kids, drop off the dry cleaning, take the dog for a walk, go for a latte, open our e-mails, and then we figure out what to have for dinner. My life is no exception; when I get home I have the same dilemma: what to make for dinner.

As a chef, the question I'm most often asked is: "Aren't you sick of cooking by the time you get home?" People are usually shocked to know that I love cooking at home and enjoy the process of turning raw ingredients into something delicious in my own kitchen.

I do admit there are times when, after years of developing and testing recipes, catering, teaching classes, cooking daily on a live TV show, and hosting more Greek family dinners than I can remember, the thought of one more trip to the grocery store is daunting. (I'm sure it's no different for you!) But no matter what, I always look forward to the next part of the journey: cooking. Actually, once I get to the grocery store or market, I'm swept up with the beautiful array of ingredients we have available. As I peruse the market aisles, I let the produce inspire

me and start imagining the various dishes I'm going to create.

Creating a delicious dinner doesn't have to be complicated: I use fairly simple cooking methods, like roasting vegetables or baking whole fish. I also take shortcuts that include roughly chopping vegetables instead of fussing over perfect cuts or using a prepared stock rather than making one from scratch. But the shortcut doesn't sacrifice the final quality of the food, it only streamlines the process. Another big factor, in taking shortcuts, is that I give myself the freedom to substitute certain ingredients. If I can't find a particular ingredient, I'll just move on to another.

There are nights when I've been shooting a show or hosting an event all day and I haven't had the time to shop. However, I'd still rather indulge in a can of sardines, some moderately stinky, creamy cheese, and a simple salad drizzled with my extra virgin olive oil than take something out of a package and reheat it. (I get a rash just thinking about all that processed food out there.) A favorite weeknight dinner is a pan-roasted fillet of halibut with grape tomatoes and a basmati rice pilaf. Although this dish takes all of 35 minutes from beginning to end, I do want to stress that it's not all about saving time. I really enjoy the cooking process and believe that it's part of the whole experience. On weekends or on special occasions, I like to flex a little more culinary muscle and make a slowly braised duck, or a lasagna made from homemade noodles.

I want to get you excited about the process of creating in your kitchen—therein lies the secret to fun—but I'd also like to spread the gospel of "Pure Food." This book—and its title—embodies my philosophy of cooking and eating well. I believe the ingredient is king, which is why I'd like you to learn as much as you can about your ingredients. You can create mouth-watering dishes every day if you start with great ingredients, which don't have to cost a million dollars or be hand-picked by Tuscan monks.

I also give you specific shopping tips to guide you when purchasing meat, fish, and produce. I'll get you asking questions so you can get to know the grocers, fishmongers, and butchers in your city or town. Once you have a relationship with these people you'll have a

better relationship with your food. Knowledge makes you a more confident shopper, and one who expects only the best. There's nothing wrong with that.

We have the most diverse supermarkets on the planet and an array of produce that is inspiring. So, in addition to favoring fresh, quality ingredients, I also introduce you to an array of ethnic ingredients that are becoming commonplace and that can add great variety to your every-day menu. After all, you can't make new friends if you always hang out with the same people! Why not try rapini or gai-lin (Chinese broccoli) instead of peas and carrots? Adding new ingredients to your repertoire will inject more adventure and fun into cooking.

The cooking methods featured in this book vary, from grilling to stir-frying and every-thing in between. The recipes are intended to introduce variety to your everyday ideas. Each will take about an hour to prepare. Some dishes are ultra quick; others take a little longer. But what I do promise you is this: Your food will taste delicious, look great, and be nutritious—and you'll be inspired to try something new every day. **Keep it fun and pure!**

a shopping, organizing & produce companion

Before we get into the specifics about shopping and ingredients, the following is the thread that weaves together all the recipes in this book. Every recipe I have developed balances these 5 very important factors. The one that is implied is fun. If I haven't said it enough, cooking is fun, it shouldn't be a chore.

1   FLAVOR, FLAVOR, FLAVOR!
2   QUALITY OF INGREDIENTS
3   IN SEASON
4   EASE OF PREPARATION
5   HEALTH

1   For me flavor is a huge priority when cooking anything for any occasion for anyone. A dish could promise to be the healthiest thing in the world, but if it doesn't taste great, I'm not interested. All these recipes taste great, otherwise, they wouldn't have made it into this book.

2   The quality of ingredients is directly tied to flavor. I believe that even if Julia Child had been presented with a stinky piece of fish, she would have fought a losing battle. And since most of us don't have Julia's culinary expertise, why not make it easy and start with fresh, flavorful ingredients that will make us stars in the kitchen? Quality doesn't necessarily mean expensive. You can, on a weekend, try some inexpensive cuts of meat for slow braising, as long as they come from good sources. This is where I employ the Italian philosophy: start with great ingredients and use simple techniques.

3   Food is seasonal, so the fact that so many people don't pay attention to this is another of my frustrations with both home cooks and restaurants alike. For some reason, we North Americans believe that produce should grow non-stop throughout the year, producing perfectly shaped, delicious produce whenever we demand it rather than in cycles, as it does naturally. Why are we compelled to buy strawberries in February? They just can't be as good as they are in the summer and they are certainly much more expensive. I'm not suggesting that we

eat turnips all winter long, but let's pay a little more attention to when nature's best is available. Many recipes in this book, where applicable, will have a suggested season for best flavor.

4   Although I'm a professional chef, my home-cooking style has been immensely streamlined over the years. I don't want you to get frustrated with overly complex recipes, so these recipes have been developed to dazzle your eyes and your taste buds yet feature fairly simple cooking techniques. That said, they do require a general level of cooking skill and will push you to refine your cooking technique. When a recipe works for both everyday dining as well as occasional entertaining, I'm ecstatic.

5   Last, but not by any means least, is health, which is the underlying principle of everything I do. I'm not talking about a diet of wheat grass and tofu. I'm thinking more holistically—how food is prepared and what we use to prepare it—for example, choosing to cook with olive oil rather than pork fat. I believe in eating a great variety of foods, in balanced measure, so our bodies don't feel deprived and tempt us into binge mode. For me, there's no substitute for real or pure products. I'd rather use less butter than start using margarine. In the same vein, I have completely eliminated soda pop from my diet: there is little nutritional value to liquid sugar, unless you're on an IV. I drink water, juice or, better still, wine.

PRODUCE COMPANION

The following entries are designed to give you a visual of some produce that you may not have tried or are not that familiar with. Flip through these pages to identify fresh produce and tips on how to cook with it.

1 **ARUGULA** • Also known as rocket or rucola, this is a bold, peppery green that's delicious in salads, on its own, or in combination with other greens, which makes for a milder, less peppery option. I always taste a leaf before using it in my salad to ensure that it's not too peppery. Look for bright green leaves that aren't wilted and be certain to wash very thoroughly in cold water until the water runs clear of sand. To maximize its freshness, don't remove stems until you're ready to wash. The ideal growing season is from spring to early winter.

2 **SHALLOTS** • These elongated purple onions have a more delicate flavor than a cooking onion, are milder to eat raw, and are essential to a French sauce. They also add a great kick to a simple dressing. Look for firm bulbs with no sprouting and smooth skin. Store in a cool, dry place; not the fridge. The shallot's peak season is spring.

3 **ESCAROLE LETTUCE** • This green—in the endive family—typically has a slightly bitter flavor although not as pronounced as Belgian endive. A hearty lettuce that holds dressing well without wilting, it's also quickly wilted in the pan. Look for light green leaves without holes and discoloration. It's usually available year round but peaks in midsummer through fall.

4 **CURLY ENDIVE** • Another member of the endive family, this green is quite bitter when eaten raw in a salad. When boiled for 2 minutes in lots of salted water, it transforms into a sweet, rich green. It's also delicious braised. In a Greek restaurant you may have had it as "horta," served with olive oil and lemon. Look for light green outer leaves with a pale yellow inner heart. The leaves have a delicately prickly outer texture that softens when cooked. Curly endive is available year round but peaks in summer through midfall.

5 **FENNEL** • A very versatile bulb with a very light creamy color and a sweet, slight flavor of anise, this vegetable is delicious raw as a crisp salad, roasted, or even grilled. Look for heavy plump bulbs that are blemish free and light colored. The bulb, stem, and inner core are eatable. Trim off the outer stems and cut as desired. Fennel is available from fall to early spring.

6 **BELGIAN ENDIVE** • A less bitter family member of endive, this uniquely cigar-shaped green is grown almost entirely in the dark, thus its light color. Because of its slight bitter bite, blending it with creamy or sweet citrus fruit creates a great harmony of flavors. Traditionally, in Europe, it's braised in a cream sauce or broth to accompany game. The endive will become more bitter if exposed to light, so store, wrapped in a paper towel and plastic, in the fridge for no more than a couple of days. Select light-colored, tightly shaped ovals without brown edges. It is available in the fall through to the end of winter.

7 **JAPANESE EGGPLANT** • This is now my favorite eggplant because it is sweet, virtually seedless, and doesn't require salting like larger eggplants. These long, light purple eggplants are available in Asian markets but also in local grocery stores. I've also discovered that they can be cooked in broth without tons of oil and still yield a creamy flesh. Pick firm, blemish-free, bright purple eggplants. Although available year round, it peaks between August and October.

8 **GINGER** • This tropical root is called a rhizome and can be used in everything from salads, stir-fries, and soups, and it even makes a great tummy-settling drink or tea. Fresh ginger, available year round, has a robust sweet but peppery flavor and should be purchased plump with smooth skin. Shriveled skin is a sign that it's dried out. When the skin is smooth and thin, you don't even need to peel it. Store it, unpeeled, in the fridge, wrapped in paper towel then plastic, for up to two weeks if fresh. Dried ginger powder is ideal for baking.

9 **BOK CHOY** • There are several varieties of this Chinese white cabbage. It requires very little cooking; all that's needed is a quick stir-fry or blanching in hot stock or water. It can be eaten raw. These greens are now grown all over the world and should be purchased when its leaves are crisp and stalks are white. The Shanghai variety is a pale sage green with pale yellow stalks. Baby bok choy can be cut in half and washed thoroughly. Store in the fridge in plastic for several days. Available year round.

10

11

12

13

14

15

16

10 GAI-LAN OR KAI-LAN • This hearty vegetable, also called Chinese broccoli, is perfect for stir-frying or can be cooked like regular broccoli. Its stems are quite thick but smooth and most varieties show cream-colored flowers. Look for dark blue-green leaves without blemishes that aren't wilted. If stems are thick, they should be peeled before cooking. Store in the fridge, wrapped in plastic for several days. It's available year round.

11 KING OYSTER MUSHROOM • Also known as eryngii, king oyster mushroom was originally from parts of the Mediterranean but introduced to Japan in recent years. This is my new favorite mushroom for grilling, roasting, or frying as it's very firm and meaty. It has a large white stem and is related to the oyster mushroom but is much less delicate. Always store mushrooms in a paper bag in the fridge to prevent drying or moisture build-up. It's available year round.

12 RAPINI • Known as broccoli rabe, rapini is an Italian broccoli with delicate leaves and a slightly bitter flavor. In the winter months, when rapini is at its peak, its flavor is milder. The best way to cook rapini is to first blanch it in rapidly boiling salted water (the bitterness intensifies if it isn't blanched) and then toss in pasta, with olive oil, or in a stir-fry. Look for flowering leaves that are plump with no blemishes and very few yellow flowers. Trim off one-third of the bottom leaves and cook as desired. It's available from autumn to late winter.

13 SWEET POTATO • There is so much confusion about yam versus sweet potato that I had to include it here. The sweet potato is a root from the morning glory family and not related to either the potato or the yam. It's crazy but it was misnamed back in the fifteenth century and to this day people confuse the two! The sweet potato is very high in vitamins A and C and has a pinky orange skin and bright orange flesh. It cooks quite quickly by roasting, boiling, or baking. Store uncooked sweet potato in a cool, dark place for up to 3 weeks. Look for firm sweet potatoes with bright-colored skin and no blemishes. Peak season is the fall through winter.

14 SWISS CHARD • This leaf is a delicious cousin of the beet and when cooked, has a flavor reminiscent of beets. Look for dark green curly leaves that are large and crisp. Chard is also available in red with a similar flavor. It needs to be thoroughly washed and can be cooked like spinach. It's great just sautéed or blanched, in a bake or a soup. When I'm out of spinach I substitute chard easily. It's also a great source of iron. It's available year round but peaks in the summer months.

15 BLOOD ORANGES • This delicious, deep-crimson variety of orange originated in Italy, specifically in Sicily. California has begun producing blood oranges as well. I've recently seen several varieties available: Moro, in particular, has a much darker crimson color and has a sweeter hint of raspberry flavor. In general, these oranges have a slight bitter edge but nothing like a grapefruit. They make incredible sauces or dressings and are delicious on a fruit plate. I look for oranges with firm flesh that feel heavy for their size. They are available in the winter to early spring.

16 KUMQUATS • These little oval citrus fruits can be eaten whole: skin, seeds, and all. They originated in Asia and work well with Asian flavor, as in a stir-fry. I also love them with duck or pork. Since the whole fruit is edible, it can be sliced and candied as a dessert garnish. The flavor is like that of orange marmalade with a little bittersweet edge. Kumquats are available from late fall to early spring.

Product Season Overview:

	SPRING	SUMMER	FALL	WINTER	
Arugula					1
Shallots					2
Escarole					3
Curly Endive					4
Fennel					5
Belgian Endive					6
Eggplant					7
Ginger					8
Bok Choy					9
Gai-lan					10
King Oyster					11
Rapini					12
Sweet Potato					13
Swiss Chard					14
Blood Oranges					15
Kumquats					16

WEEKEND PROJECT: GETTING ORGANIZED

I must confess, organization is not my strong suit. But, I have pushed myself to keep my kitchen organized, and it really reduces my prep time and keeps me from throwing pots around when I can't find something I need. If I can get it together, then you can too.

DRY STORAGE

I've found this cool system of organizing my dry ingredients—you know the 17 types of flour—in shallow, rectangular clip-down containers. I label them facing out and stack them for easy retrieval and a neat look. Why is this going to make you a better cook? When you're saving time looking for ingredients and you can easily glance at your cupboard to get a snap-shot of what your pantry holds, the cooking is more enjoyable and easier to accomplish. The added bonus is that you can immediately see what is running low because the containers are see-through. This system is an organization guru's dream and the too busy, somewhat messy person's savior.

Similar systems can be set up for pasta, rice, and even your fridge. If you prefer glass, try using Mason jars or even recycled jars that you re-label.

SHOPPING

At points in my life I've found myself searching frantically for ingredients, running like a lunatic from store to store trying to locate such things as pear leaves for a photo shoot, or having to cram groceries in the back of my van until the last box was overflowing. I've now figured out ways to make my food-shopping experience less stressful and more enjoyable: since it must be done,

- I find the stores in my neighborhood that are open late and I try to do my staple shopping during those later, "off" hours. The lineups are slim and I can whip through the store with ease.
- One of the most important factors is to know what types of stores are best for certain ingredients. It sounds like a no-brainer, but I've spent countless wasted hours in the past on scavenger hunts for ingredients that weren't even available in those stores.
- I always scope out the stores in my neighborhood first to determine if they have the majority of things I like. I'm very particular about my meat and fish so I like to either find a food shop that has good quality proteins and staff that are knowledgeable or I prefer

to visit my local fishmonger and butcher shop when I have the time. I have found a little bit of extra research at the beginning saves me time and money, and it ensures that I'm satisfied with the quality of a product.

- Once I have my target food stores, I select a few ethnic ones for my special-occasion shopping. For me, the main course always dictates what stores I'll be shopping at. If I feel like making a duck breast entrée, for instance, I'll choose the best location for duck and get my produce and other ingredients there as well.

Since I like to shop for fresh ingredients every couple of days, I make sure that the vegetable section in my fridge is stocked well and that—more importantly—my pantry has a full assortment of goodies to choose from. I also use my freezer as a place to store my must-haves for the week. The following are a few of my suggestions for a well-stocked kitchen:

PANTRY BOOSTERS

Canned tuna • I look for albacore, a whole, white canned tuna that comes from better quality fish, and which is firm and ideal for a quick protein addition to any salad.

Sockeye salmon • This is a firm, fatty, deep-orange variety of West Coast salmon that's loaded with flavor. I often add it to salads for dinner.

Canned assorted beans • Use canned beans in a quick soup or salad, or as part of a stew.

Tamari soy sauce • This Japanese-style soy sauce adds great depth of flavor and offers less sodium than traditional soy sauce. The name "tamari," actually refers to a style of brewing soy sauce, not a brand.

Smoked paprika • I'm hooked on this smoky, burnt-orange dried pepper. It's great for chicken and pork.

Maldon sea salt • From Maldon, England, this sea salt is shaved for a mild delicate flavor and interesting texture. I use it as a finishing salt.

Fleur de sel • Fleur de sel is a coarse gray sea salt with a mineral taste; I also use this as a finishing salt.

Good quality light coconut milk • This gives you the rich taste of coconut milk with less fat.

Good quality prepared tomato sauce • Once I've found a prepared tomato sauce I like, I use it in stews, over pasta, or even as a soup. It's the ultimate time saver.

Extra virgin olive oil • Using extra virgin olive oil is a great way to add flavor with a peppery kick. Its health benefits include lowering cholesterol and reducing blood pressure.

Basmati rice • This is a delicious, nutty rice that cooks in 12 minutes.

Mixed dried nuts and fruit • I always keep a stash of dried fruit and nuts in my pantry for breakfast, to add to desserts, or as a healthy snack.

Pomegranate molasses • This is a great sweet-and-sour elixir for dressings, sauces, and drizzles. It's available in gourmet and Middle Eastern food stores.

Maple syrup • This cooked, reduced tree sap is less sweet than honey and is ideal for barbecue sauces, smoothies, or in yogurt.

FRIDGE

Dijon mustard • Dijon mustard is the spicy key to making any salad dressing perfect. It also helps to bind the oil and vinegar.

Toasted sesame oil • This oil adds great depth of flavor to fish or a simple stir-fry.

Thai curry paste • Thai curry paste has all the flavorful, hard-to-find ingredients in one little jar.

Whole vanilla pods • Vanilla beans are my one absolute must-have for custards, muffins, flavoring sugar, or a simple sauce.

Assortment of good quality cheeses • Cheese makes for a great appetizer in a flash.

Good quality olives • Olives keep people busy eating while you're preparing something more substantial.

Miso • Miso is found in health-food stores. This fermented salty boost of flavor makes a perfect crust on lamb or fish.

Plain Balkan-style yogurt • Yogurt is perfect for dressing or as a quick dessert, or drain and use instead of sour cream.

FREEZER

Edamame • Young soy beans; edamame are quick and easy to steam for a side dish in minutes.

Bags of berries • Berries are great for morning smoothies, quick crisps, or muffins.

Phyllo pastry • Phyllo is great for making quick hors d'œuvres or quick strudels.

Assorted broths • Chicken, vegetable, beef, and fish broth are a great foundation for making quick soups or using to flavor rice dishes.

Brown, over-ripe bananas • These are perfect for muffins or breads.

SEAFOOD

Seafood is a huge part of my diet and I have found two or three favorite spots in my city to purchase it. Here the "pure" food philosophy is obvious. Starting with a fresh piece of fish is the best way to enjoy the delicious recipes in this book. I suggest that you find a store or fishmonger in your neighborhood, introduce yourself, and ask a ton of questions. Once a store owner or clerk recognizes you and knows you come in often, he or she will be more likely to ensure that you get great quality seafood. Test the fish market's product for quality. Ask the fishmonger what days certain fish come in so you know when to put it on your menu. In some cases, stores only get deliveries once a week. That means when you buy fish on a Saturday, you may be buying fish that came in on Tuesday. It's best to ask. Another very important question is "Has the fish been previously frozen?" Sometimes fish are flash-frozen right at sea and can yield a superior product to fresh fish that's been lying around for a week. If you buy a previously frozen fish, never refreeze it.

Another big no-no are fish markets that leave their fish out in the sun in the middle of summer. I stay away from those.

I always ask to smell the fish. It's better for them to give you a funny look then for you to go home with stinky fish. Fish should never smell stinky. When you eat sushi, the fish has been out of the water for a short period of time, and it hasn't started to spoil yet. That's why sushi can be eaten raw and has a clean smell of the sea. If you plan on making any fish that is either just marinated or served very rare, make sure to ask for sushi grade. Cooking fish, especially oily varieties like mackerel, sardines, or even salmon, will produce a smell in your kitchen from the oils the fish renders. I always have my stove vent on high and open a window—if possible—to minimize this effect.

When you buy a very fresh piece of fish, it can easily stay in your fridge for a couple of days before cooking. Just ensure that you place it in the coldest part of your fridge (the meat drawers), well wrapped in plastic. In general, it's better to select a whole fish and ask the fishmonger to cut it on the spot because once the fish is cut, there is more surface area exposed, and it deteriorates much more quickly.

Here are the other ways to ensure that your fish is fresh. Ask your fishmonger, with gloves on, to show you the following:

1   Eyes that are bright and plump, not sunken
2   Gills that are bright red
3   For certain fish like trout, that the slimy film on the skin is plentiful (slime is good)
4   The flesh is firm to touch and won't leave a print if you press with your finger
5   If fish is filleted, that it is intact, not breaking apart

A very current issue on people's minds is farmed fish versus wild fish. It's a very complex issue, but again I urge you to have a variety of fish on your menu and not stick to just one. Our waters are very diverse, but we tend to eat in fashionable trends and we over-fish certain species. Salmon, for example, is meant to have a season in the wild. It spawns at certain times of the year and is available fresh in the spring. Wild salmon will generally have a much richer pink color, due to the crustaceans it feeds on, than its farmed counterpart. The reality is that there's just not enough wild fish in the sea to feed the world. I think we should consider making lifestyle changes and get used to a variety of different fish and that some farmed fish is to be expected. Some parts of the world have better farming practices than others, but that's another book.

If you want more information about the species of fish that are endangered, there are several websites that list these. You can do a search on "sustainable fish" or on "restaurant associations for sustainable fishing" for your area.

MEAT

Meat definitely deserves more of our attention these days. I have become very particular about the quality of my meat because it can vary dramatically. I like to be informed about where my meat comes from and how it's fed. Just recently I discovered an amazing butcher who specializes in lamb and goat. He recently sold me one of the most delicious cuts of fresh lamb I have ever eaten. As I chatted with him, he explained how he judges sheep at the Royal Winter Fair. Needless to say, I will probably go back because this butcher knows when the meat arrived and which farmer raised it, and he will insist on the best quality. Of course these more lengthy excursions are saved for a day when I have time to spare.

You have probably noticed that the flavor of two like cuts of meat will be quite different, depending on where they came from and how they were stored. This is how steak houses brand their reputations. The magic of a great steak house is in the quality of the meat, how long it's aged, and if the chef knows how to cook it. Assuming you know how to cook steak, all you have to worry about is the first two factors.

Aged beef is hard to come by in the traditional grocery store because the process of aging can take several weeks and costs the supplier a great deal of money. The meat will also lose about 20 percent of its original weight, also reducing its value. Aging the beef not only gives it a more pronounced flavor, but tenderizes it as well. I am now less likely to go to a steak house and dish out huge bucks but instead will go to a butcher and ask for aged meat and prepare it at home when I can.

I'd rather eat less, if it's a well-fed, well-aged piece of beef, than more if it's a tough, flavorless cut—and one that is potentially a health risk—that happens to be on sale. Further to this, some new butcher shops are popping up, in niche markets, offering boutique services. I recently saw one that posts all the farmers names on chalk boards that correspond with their current stock. This way the consumer has a path directly from the purchase point right to the farm. It's quite an appealing service, if you value the quality and attention required to raise a delicious and nutritious piece of meat.

Needless to say, these are boutique operations that can't produce beef for the whole world, so I suggest making a contact at your local grocery store butcher's counter or market, and try a few before settling on one.

POULTRY

There's been much confusion of late with the labeling of meat, and poultry is no exception. The choices presented to you usually include organic, free-range, or grain fed. Aren't we all confused? My advice on this subject is to ask a lot of questions about each label, wherever you shop.

I recommend finding butchers whose chickens are fed a richer grain variety for the best quality. In the grocery store, look for any sign noting "no hormones." Another thing to look for on the label is the "air-chilled" sign. This label ensures that the bird hasn't been immersed in cold water—a process that injects water into the flesh, creating birds that weigh more but which are full of water.

Organic chicken, which is becoming more commonplace, is often twice the price of an average chicken. This extra ten dollars or so spent tells you that the chicken is naturally fed a rich grain mixture, had room to roam, and is hormone and antibiotic free. It will also be slightly larger because it's had a slower growing process. As far as flavor goes, some people find it difficult to tell the difference between organic and non-organic. The flavor comes more from what the chicken eats and not whether it's fed antibiotics. The choice is yours.

Now that the shopping is out of the way, let's start the fun part: Cooking!

No matter what day of the week, there's always a salad on my table. When I'm having a busy week and feeling exhausted, I clean out the fridge and the cupboards and put out a salad and starter feast full of dips, tuna, salmon, beans, and more. It's so delicious with tons of variety. And I feel like I'm doing a good deed…you know, eating lighter and cleaning out the fridge at the same time.

I'm truly mesmerized by the variety of produce that we have available in our local markets (I swear sometimes the fruits and vegetables call me to pick them up and take them home). It's this variety that keeps me inspired through the seasons.

I like to wow guests, or even myself, by mastering a new combination of flavors that becomes a conversation piece simply because people expect fairly predictable salads.

In this chapter, featuring so many great starters and salads, and with so many interesting new combinations, you can really have fun and capture the best flavors by eating in season.

salads, dips & starters

CRISPY OLIVE OIL CRACKERS

These snappy crackers take about 30 minutes—including baking time —and the fat comes strictly from the extra virgin olive oil, which also gives the crackers its peppery kick. They are perfect for an impromptu dinner get-together and can be topped with any of the dips in this book, or with your favorite cheeses.

PREP TIME • 20 minutes
BAKING TIME • 15 minutes
SEASON • all seasons

¾ cup unbleached all-purpose flour + 2 Tbsp (175 mL)
¼ cup fine semolina (60 mL)
¼ tsp salt (1 mL)
¼ tsp baking soda (1 mL)
¼ tsp cracked black peppercorns (1 mL)
3 Tbsp olive oil (45 mL)
1 Tbsp sesame seeds (15 mL)
¼ cup buttermilk (60 mL)
1 egg white + 1 tsp water (5 mL), whisked together
Coarse sea salt

Preheat the oven to 375°F (190°C).

Combine the dry ingredients in the food processor. Add the olive oil and pulse until the mixture resembles coarse meal. Transfer the mixture to a bowl and add the sesame seeds. Stir in the buttermilk; continue stirring until the mixture comes together.

Turn the mixture onto a lightly floured surface. Knead several times until the dough forms a ball. If the dough is sticky, sprinkle lightly with flour. Roll out the dough very thinly into a 10- x 12-inch rectangle. Using a crimped pastry wheel or a knife, cut the dough into a grid pattern, creating about thirty 2- x 2-inch rectangles. Line a baking sheet with parchment paper. Place the rectangles on the baking sheet, and brush each with the egg and water mixture. Sprinkle with salt and bake for 12 to 15 minutes until browned and crisp. Set aside to cool before serving.

< MAKES ABOUT 30 CRACKERS >

YELLOW PEPPER AND CREAM CHEESE DIP

This is one deliciously creamy possibility to accompany the Crispy Olive Oil Crackers on page 30. The dip comes together in a flash once the peppers are roasted. You can also substitute deli-counter-bought roasted red peppers to save some time. The final dip, which has a sunshine-yellow color, could also accompany grilled asparagus or any other grilled veggies.

PREP TIME • 10 minutes
COOKING TIME • 35 minutes
SEASON • all seasons

2 yellow bell peppers

8 oz Danish-style cream cheese (250 g)

2 Tbsp chopped fresh dill, plus 1 sprig for garnish (30 mL)

1 Tbsp freshly squeezed lime juice (15 mL)

Sea salt and freshly cracked black peppercorns

Pinch cayenne, optional

Crispy Olive Oil Crackers, for dipping (see p. 30)

Preheat the oven to 400°F (200°C).

Roast the peppers on a baking sheet until soft and slightly charred, about 35 minutes, turning them halfway through the cooking time.

Transfer the roasted peppers to a bowl and cover with plastic for about 5 minutes to steam (the steam will help loosen the peppers' charred skin). Once the peppers are cool enough to handle, remove the skin and discard along with the seeds and stem. Put the peeled, roasted peppers in a food processor and pulse until puréed. Add the cream cheese, dill, lime juice, salt, pepper, and cayenne to taste; pulse until combined. Serve with the Crispy Olive Oil Crackers, bread, or grilled vegetables.

< MAKES ABOUT 1½ CUPS OR 8 SERVINGS >

TOASTED WALNUT AND RED PEPPER SPREAD

This is an unusual dip inspired by the flavors of Spain. The toasted nuts add a creamy, rich texture to the roasted pepper spread, while the molasses gives it a perfect sweet-and-sour balance.

PREP TIME • 10 minutes
BAKING TIME • 40 minutes
SEASON • all seasons

1 red bell pepper

2 small shallots, peeled

Extra virgin olive oil for drizzling

¼ cup walnuts (60 mL)

½-inch-thick slice rustic bread, about 4 inches
    in diameter, crust removed

1 tsp pomegranate molasses or sherry vinegar (5 mL)

⅓ cup extra virgin olive oil (75 mL)

Pinch cayenne

Sea salt and freshly cracked black peppercorns

Preheat the oven to 400°F (200°C).

Roast the pepper and shallots, drizzled with a little olive oil, on a small baking dish in the oven for about 35 minutes. Turn occasionally to char evenly.

While the vegetables are roasting, on a separate baking sheet toast the walnuts in the oven for about 4 minutes or until just golden. Remove the walnuts and set aside. Place the bread directly on a rack in the oven and toast for 5 minutes or until just crisp. Remove the toast and set aside to cool.

Transfer the roasted peppers to a bowl and cover with plastic for about 5 minutes to steam (the steam will help loosen the peppers' charred skin). Once the peppers are cool enough to handle, remove the skin and discard along with the seeds and stem. Put the peeled, roasted peppers, and the shallots in a food processor and pulse until puréed. Add the walnuts and pulse several times until just crushed. Add the vinegar or molasses, and the olive oil in two stages while the motor is pulsing.

Season with the cayenne, and the salt and cracked peppercorns to taste; serve with Crispy Olive Oil Crackers (see p. 30).

< MAKES ABOUT 1 CUP OR 8 SERVINGS >

WATERCRESS, APPLE AND PECAN SALAD

This recipe is the ideal example of how I love my salads: with color, nuts, and great flavor contrast. The crisp Granny Smith apples add a delicious tart accent to this blend. It's also great with pears.

PREP TIME • 25 minutes
COOKING TIME • none
SEASON • fall

1 small bunch watercress, washed and stemmed
One 5-oz (150-g) pkg mixed organic greens
1 small Granny Smith apple, peeled, cored, and diced
½ lemon
¼ cup pecan halves (60 mL)

Dressing

1 shallot, minced
1 tsp Dijon mustard (5 mL)
3 Tbsp sherry vinegar (45 mL)
1 tsp honey (5 mL)
⅓ cup toasted peanut oil (75 mL) or grape seed oil
Sea salt and freshly cracked black peppercorns

Dry the greens in a salad spinner or pat dry with a cloth.

Combine the shallot, Dijon mustard, sherry vinegar, honey, peanut oil, salt, and pepper in a small food processor and pulse until smooth. Adjust the seasoning to taste.

In a small bowl, squeeze the lemon over the diced apple to prevent it from discoloring; set aside.

In a large bowl, combine the mixed greens, watercress, and apple. Toss with half the dressing (reserve any leftover dressing for serving at the table). If the salad seems too dry, add more dressing. Sprinkle with pecans and serve immediately.

< MAKES 4 TO 6 SERVINGS >

GRILLED ASPARAGUS WITH SMOKED PAPRIKA AÏOLI

"Aïoli" is a great word used in the south of France for a homemade garlic mayonnaise. I love the rich taste! This recipe features spring-fresh asparagus grilled until crisp on the outside and just tender inside. For contrast, the bold aïoli hits you with a smoky garlic punch. If you would rather not eat raw yolks, you can always buy prepared mayonnaise and add the garlic, lemon, and paprika for a similar flavor. If making your own aïoli, refrigerate immediately and serve only on the day of preparation. The prepared version will keep several days in the fridge.

PREP TIME • 10 minutes
COOKING TIME • 5 minutes
SEASON • spring

1 lb thin asparagus, trimmed about 2 inches
    from the bottom (500 g)
Sea salt and freshly cracked black peppercorns

Aïoli
1 clove garlic, minced
½ tsp salt (2 mL)
½ tsp Dijon mustard (2 mL)
1 egg yolk
Juice of ½ lemon
½ tsp smoked paprika (2 mL)
Pinch cayenne
⅓ cup extra virgin olive oil (75 mL)

Preheat barbecue to medium high. Grill asparagus for 4 to 5 minutes across or adjacent to the direction of barbecue grill (to prevent asparagus from falling in). Roll several times until lightly browned. Sprinkle with salt and pepper and transfer to plate.

In a food processor, add the minced garlic, salt, mustard, yolk, lemon juice, paprika, and cayenne; pulse until combined. (If available, use the small insert for a food processor.)

With the motor still running, slowly add the olive oil in a steady stream through the spout.

To serve, drizzle the asparagus with the aïoli or serve on the side in a bowl for dipping.

< MAKES ABOUT ½ CUP AÏOLI OR 4 TO 6 SERVINGS >

JAPANESE EGGPLANT ROLLS WITH BLEU D'AUVERGNE

This is a dynamite appetizer roll that melts in your mouth with a burst of sweet, creamy contrasts in flavor. I'm suggesting this fabulous blue because it's my latest craze but any Québécois blue cheese would also be great. The Japanese eggplant has a brilliant purple blast of color, is less bitter, and has very few seeds compared to the traditional eggplant. The key is to bathe it in olive oil and roast until golden and soft. All of the preparation can be done in advance and assembled when you like. The rolls are best served at room temperature.

PREP TIME • 20 minutes
COOKING TIME • 25 minutes
SEASON • summer/fall

1 large Japanese eggplant
Olive oil, for drizzling
Sea salt and freshly cracked black peppercorns

Pesto

1 small bunch fresh parsley, roughly chopped
1 large handful of fresh basil leaves, roughly chopped
¼ cup toasted pine nuts (60 mL)
¼ cup extra virgin olive oil (60 mL)
Sea salt and freshly cracked black peppercorns
1 roasted red bell pepper, peeled, seeded, and thinly sliced
   (for roasting instructions, see p. 31)
3 oz bleu d'Auvergne or other creamy blue cheese (75 g)

Preheat the oven to 375°F (190°C).

Cut the eggplant in half. Slice each half lengthwise into ¼-inch-thick slices. You should have about 12 slices. Drizzle a baking dish or sheet with olive oil and arrange the slices in a single layer. Drizzle the eggplant slices with oil. Sprinkle with salt and pepper to taste. Roast for about 25 minutes or until golden and just soft. Remove and cool slightly.

Meanwhile, in a food processor, combine the parsley, basil, pine nuts, and olive oil until it has the consistency of a paste or pesto. Season with salt and pepper to taste. Spread a thin layer of the parsley pesto on the slices of eggplant. Add a layer of the roasted red pepper, arranging horizontally so that the pepper extends beyond the edges of each eggplant slice. In the center of each stacked eggplant slice, place a bite-size piece of blue cheese. Starting from one end, tightly roll each eggplant slice away from you and secure with a toothpick.

< MAKES 12 EGGPLANT ROLLS >

SPANISH-STYLE POTATO FRITTATA WITH SMOKED SALMON

A flight attendant, named Christina, inspired this recipe while I was on a cross-country appearance. She handed me a little hand-written note and told me that she watched my television show and this was one of her favorite tapas. I adapted her recipe by reducing the oil significantly and added some smoked salmon. Prepare it for lunch or as a great little appetizer. The colors in this frittata are particularly vibrant. Viva España!

PREP TIME • 15 minutes
COOKING TIME • 25 minutes
SEASON • all seasons

3 medium Yukon Gold potatoes,
    peeled and diced (about 1 lb/500 g)
1 small onion, chopped
1 red bell pepper, seeded and diced
5 eggs, beaten and seasoned
¼ cup extra virgin olive oil (60 mL)
1 Tbsp chopped fresh chervil or dill (15 mL)
5 oz thinly sliced smoked salmon (150 g)
2 Tbsp sour cream (30 mL)
Sea salt and freshly cracked black peppercorns

Preheat the oven to 325°F (160°C).

In a deep 10½-inch ovenproof skillet, heat the oil on medium until hot but not smoking. Add the potatoes, season with salt and pepper, and cook for about 9 to 11 minutes or until the potatoes are golden and cooked through.

Add the onion and bell pepper to the skillet and toss for 3 minutes or until the pepper is just tender.

Add the seasoned eggs and chives to cover the potato mixture. Transfer the pan to the oven and bake for 10 minutes or until the frittata is set. Serve with slices of smoked salmon, and top with sour cream and sprigs of chervil or dill.

< MAKES 6 SERVINGS >

TOMATO-OLIVE MINT SALAD

The taste of this salad hinges fully on the quality and flavor of the tomatoes and olive oil. As you can see from the main ingredients, there isn't much else to it. The flavors are North African, where the combination of fresh mint, salty olives, and ripe tomatoes sing in perfect harmony.

PREP TIME • 15 minutes
COOKING TIME • none
SEASON • summer

3 medium field tomatoes, cut into 2-inch chunks

1 red onion, thinly sliced

⅓ cup cured black olives (75 mL)

1 clove garlic, minced

¼ cup good quality extra virgin olive oil (60 mL)

1 Tbsp sherry vinegar (15 mL)

Freshly cracked black peppercorns

¼ cup chopped fresh mint leaves (60 mL)

Sea salt

Combine all the salad ingredients in a medium bowl. Toss to combine. For the best flavor, let stand for 30 minutes while you prepare the rest of your meal.

< MAKES 4 SERVINGS >

LEAN HERB SALAD

Adding whole herbs to greens really boosts a salad's flavor. The dressing on this salad is lean, with just a touch of olive oil. It's perfectly refreshing for summer with just about anything on the barbecue. Choose any soft, leafy fresh herbs you like to substitute for those you don't.

PREP TIME • 15 minutes
COOKING TIME • none
SEASON • summer/fall

1 handful fresh basil leaves or Thai basil leaves
Several sprigs fresh cilantro
4 cups loosely packed mixed greens (1 L)

Dressing
Juice of 1 lime
3 Tbsp rice wine vinegar (45 mL)
3 Tbsp unsweetened apple juice (45 mL)
2 tsp honey (10 mL)
2 tsp Dijon mustard (10 mL)
1 Tbsp tamari soy sauce (15 mL)
Sea salt and freshly cracked black peppercorns
3 Tbsp extra virgin olive oil (45 mL)

In a large bowl, add the basil and cilantro to the salad greens and toss to blend.

To make the dressing, in a small bowl whisk together the lime juice, rice vinegar, apple juice, honey, Dijon, tamari soy sauce, salt, and pepper. Whisk in the olive oil and add the dressing to the bowl of greens. Toss to combine and serve.

< MAKES 4 SERVINGS >

ARUGULA AND SPINACH SALAD WITH CARAMELIZED SHALLOTS

This salad is a sophisticated variation on a Greek salad. The sweetness of the caramelized shallots is a perfect contrast to the peppery arugula and salty feta. Although the recipe calls for using packaged and pre-washed organic arugula and spinach, I recommend washing the greens yourself before adding to the salad. (In the summer when local produce is available on its stem, it usually holds lots of dirt so it needs to be washed thoroughly.)

PREP TIME • 10 minutes
COOKING TIME • 8 minutes
SEASON • summer

½ of a 5-oz pkg (150-g) baby arugula, washed

½ of a 5-oz pkg (150-g) baby spinach, washed

3 oz Greek creamy feta cheese (90 g), crumbled

1 Tbsp extra virgin olive oil (15 mL)

2 large shallots, thinly sliced

2 Tbsp sherry or red wine vinegar (30 mL)

¼ cup extra virgin olive oil (60 mL)

1 tsp Dijon mustard (5 mL)

½ tsp dried Greek oregano (2 mL)

Sea salt

Warm the olive oil in a small skillet over medium heat. Add the sliced shallots and stir frequently for about 6 to 8 minutes or until golden. Reduce the heat to low and cook for a further 2 minutes until gently browned. Remove from heat and set aside.

Meanwhile, wash and dry the arugula and spinach; place in a medium bowl.

To make the dressing, whisk together the vinegar, mustard, and oregano in a small bowl. Continue whisking while slowly pouring in the oil until well combined. Season with salt.

Gently toss the greens with the cheese and vinaigrette to coat. Sprinkle with caramelized shallots and serve.

< MAKES 4 TO 6 SERVINGS >

PANCETTA, LETTUCE AND TOMATO SALAD — AKA "PLT SALAD"

I was having a little fun with the traditional bacon lettuce tomato combination in this recipe. This salad is like a BLT sandwich without the bread. I also like using pancetta (Italian bacon) so I've called it a PLT. (All this explanation for just a simple salad!) It's soooo good.

PREP TIME • 15 minutes
COOKING TIME • 5 minutes
SEASON • summer

1 head Boston (bibb) lettuce, washed and pulled apart into leaves

4 thin slices pancetta, fried and drained on paper towel

¼ cup extra virgin olive oil (60 mL)

2 Tbsp apple cider vinegar (30 mL)

Juice of ½ lime

2 Tbsp mayonnaise (30 mL)

4 chives, finely chopped

Sea salt and freshly cracked black peppercorns

20 grape tomatoes, cut in half

1 small ripe avocado, peeled, pitted, and diced

Spin the washed, whole lettuce leaves carefully to dry but not bruise. Arrange in a large but shallow salad bowl.

In a medium bowl, whisk together the olive oil, cider vinegar, lime juice, mayonnaise, chives, salt, and pepper. Add the grape tomatoes and diced avocado and gently toss to thoroughly coat.

Spoon this mixture onto the lettuce leaves, covering evenly. Arrange the pancetta slices so that they are tucked in among the leaves. When ready to serve, place a bundle of leaves, the mixed vegetables, and a pancetta slice on each plate.

< MAKES 4 SERVINGS >

SPICY BEEF SALAD

Once you taste this zesty bold salad, you won't believe that the only fat in it comes from the filet mignon and 1 teaspoon of oil used for grilling. Both the Thai chili peppers and basil are available in Asian grocery stores but feel free to substitute with any type of chili pepper and with regular basil. If available, you can also add ripe green mangoes to this salad. Spicy Beef Salad is perfect for serving in the summer and fall months because it's very refreshing, and everything is done on the barbecue.

PREP TIME • 15 minutes
COOKING TIME • 8 minutes
SEASON • summer/fall

½ lb filet mignon, one inch thick (250 g)
Sea salt and freshly cracked black peppercorns
1 tsp vegetable oil (5 mL)
1 Thai chili pepper, finely chopped, or chili flakes
One 5-oz (150-g) pkg mixed baby greens
½ cup fresh cilantro leaves (125 mL)
½ cup Thai basil leaves (125 mL)
1 red onion, cut in half and thinly sliced

Dressing

¼ cup freshly squeezed lime juice (60 mL)
2 Tbsp fish sauce (30 mL)
2 tsp granulated sugar (10 mL)
½ tsp freshly cracked black peppercorns (2 mL)
¼ cup each chopped salted peanuts and
    Thai basil leaves (60 mL), for garnish

Preheat a grill on high. Brush the filet mignon with vegetable oil; season with salt and pepper, and sprinkle with chopped Thai chili pepper. Grill the beef to medium rare, about 4 minutes per side. Remove from the grill and set aside for 5 minutes.

For the dressing, whisk together all the ingredients in a small bowl. Set aside until ready to serve.

Combine the mixed greens, cilantro, basil, and red onion in a large bowl.

When ready to serve, slice the filet into ⅛-inch-thick slices and add to the greens. Pour in the dressing and toss to combine. Garnish with peanuts and Thai basil sprigs before serving.

< MAKES 4 SERVINGS >

POTATO AND EDAMAME SALAD

The addition of edamame (green soybeans) to potato salad is a great way to give a crunchy texture and to add both fiber and iron. You can find frozen edamame at most supermarkets and at Asian grocery stores.

PREP TIME • 20 minutes
COOKING TIME • 20 minutes
SEASON • all seasons

½ lb frozen edamame, shelled (250 g)

2 lb fingerling potatoes or red new potatoes, cut into quarters (1 kg)

2 tsp Dijon mustard (10 mL)

Juice of 1 lime

¼ cup extra virgin olive oil (60 mL)

1 tsp minced garlic (5 mL)

¼ tsp minced fresh ginger (1 mL)

2 scallions, thinly sliced

1 Tbsp chopped fresh cilantro (15 mL)

Sea salt and freshly cracked black peppercorns

2 oz pancetta, finely chopped and fried until crisp, for garnish (50 g)

In a medium pot over high, add the potatoes and enough cold, salted water to cover the potatoes by 1 inch; bring to a boil. Reduce heat to medium low and simmer for about 13 to 16 minutes or until tender. At the 12 minute point of cooking, when the potatoes are almost tender, add the shelled edamame. Cook for a further 3 minutes or until both are tender. Drain and cool slightly in a medium bowl.

Meanwhile, in a small bowl, whisk together the remaining ingredients except the pancetta. Pour this mixture over the drained but still warm potatoes and edamame and toss to combine. Season with salt and cracked peppercorns and garnish with chopped crisp pancetta before serving.

< MAKES 6 SERVINGS >

URBAN DINNER SALAD

I've made this kind of salad for dinner umpteen times. It's versatile, depending on what's in your pantry or what season you're serving it in. Use leftover chicken, canned tuna, or salmon for more protein.

PREP TIME • 20 minutes
COOKING TIME • 20 minutes
SEASON • all seasons

4 medium red new potatoes, skin on and quartered

1 lb French green beans, trimmed (500 g)

2 large eggs, hard boiled for 8 minutes and quartered

2 small tomatoes, cut into wedges (only in summer)

Dressing

¼ tsp fennel seeds (1mL)

½ tsp coriander seeds (2 mL)

¼ cup extra virgin olive oil (60 mL)

Grated zest of 1 lemon

Juice of 1 lemon

1 tsp Worcestershire sauce (5 mL)

1 clove garlic, minced

½ tsp capers (2 mL)

2 tsp Dijon mustard (10 mL)

Sea salt and freshly cracked black peppercorns

Garnish

2 green onions, sliced

½ bunch fresh parsley, chopped

Cook the potatoes in a large pot of boiling salted water for 20 minutes or until tender. At the 18-minute mark, when the potatoes are almost tender, add the green beans and cook them together until the potatoes are completely cooked (this means one less pot to clean). Drain the vegetables and cool slightly before transferring to a serving bowl. While still warm, pour half the dressing over the vegetables and toss gently.

Meanwhile, to make the dressing, pound the seeds with a mortar and pestle until coarsely ground. In a small bowl, add the ground seeds to the remaining ingredients and whisk to combine.

To serve, arrange the protein of your choice (meat or fish) over the tomatoes, eggs, beans, and potatoes. Pour the remaining dressing overtop and adjust the seasoning to taste. Sprinkle with green onions and chopped parsley, and serve at room temperature.

< MAKES 4 TO 6 SERVINGS >

SWEET POTATO, ORANGE AND BELGIAN ENDIVE SALAD

This colorful salad combines the delicious flavors and many shades of fall. The gentle peppery notes of the extra virgin olive oil are a perfect contrast to the sweet potatoes. The orange provides a refreshing burst of citrus flavor. I assemble this salad by layering the ingredients to keep all the flavors evenly distributed.

PREP TIME • 20 minutes
COOKING TIME • 15 minutes
SEASON • fall/winter

1 medium sweet potato, peeled and cut into ½ inch dice
¼ cup extra virgin olive oil (60 mL)
Sea salt and freshly cracked black peppercorns
2 fresh sage leaves, finely chopped
2 medium navel oranges, peeled and chopped into segments
    (reserve the juice)
1 tsp Dijon mustard (5 mL)
2 Tbsp balsamic vinegar (30 mL)
Grated zest of 1 orange
1 small shallot, finely chopped
2 heads Belgian endive, trimmed

Preheat the oven to 375°F (190°C).

In a large bowl, toss the sweet potato with 1 Tbsp olive oil, chopped sage, and sea salt and pepper to taste. Spread the coated sweet potatoes onto a baking sheet and roast for 14 to 16 minutes or until tender and golden. Remove from the oven and let cool.

Meanwhile, in a medium bowl, whisk together the reserved orange juice, the remaining olive oil, the mustard, balsamic vinegar, orange rind, and the shallot until smooth. Adjust the seasoning and set aside.

Pull apart the leaves of the endive, keeping their boat shape. In a shallow, 11 inch (28 cm) oval serving dish, arrange the first layer of leaves into a fan pattern, starting at one end of the dish. Sprinkle with the cooled sweet potato pieces and with several orange segments; drizzle with some of the dressing. Keep repeating this process, moving down the dish, to form several endive fans topped with vegetables and dressing until all the ingredients are used. Drizzle with any leftover dressing and serve immediately.

< MAKES 4 TO 6 SERVINGS >

WARM APPLE AND FENNEL SALAD

This is my kind of salad: crunchy, tangy, and light with a sweet finish of warm apples. I always use a firm apple that keeps a bit of texture when cooked. It's a soothing fall and winter salad that has nothing green. I'm known for making tart dressings, so if you like a sweeter taste, reduce the vinegar by half.

PREP TIME • 20 minutes
COOKING TIME • 10 minutes
SEASON • fall/winter

½ fennel bulb, core removed and finely sliced

2 carrots, julienned

1 head Belgian endive, sliced

2 shallots, sliced

2 Spy or Fuji apples, each cored and cut into 12 wedges

¼ cup extra virgin olive oil (60 mL)

Pinch ground cinnamon

Pinch ground allspice

¼ tsp ground fennel seeds (1 mL)

¼ tsp mustard powder (1 mL)

¼ cup apple cider vinegar (60 mL)

¼ cup apple cider (60 mL)

Sea salt and freshly cracked black peppercorns

Combine the fennel, carrots, and endive in a large bowl and toss well.

In a large skillet, heat ½ the oil on medium. Add the shallots and sauté until soft, about 3 to 5 minutes. Increase the heat to high and add the apples; sauté for a further 4 to 6 minutes or until just softened. Add the allspice and cinnamon and toss. Remove the skillet from the heat and set aside.

To make the dressing, whisk together the fennel seeds, mustard powder, cider vinegar, cider, remaining olive oil, salt, and pepper until well combined.

Remove the apples from the skillet and arrange overtop the fennel, carrots, and endive. Transfer the dressing into the skillet to warm, stirring gently. Pour the warmed dressing overtop the apple salad and toss. Serve immediately while still warm.

< MAKES 6 SERVINGS >

ESCAROLE, POMEGRANATE AND GRAPEFRUIT SALAD

Escarole is my choice for a hearty salad because it holds its shape and doesn't wilt after dressing. The eye-candy factor and the taste combination of grapefruit and pomegranates are great for the holidays, when both are in season. In spring, summer, and fall, use other seasonal veggies.

PREP TIME • 25 minutes
COOKING TIME • none
SEASON • winter

1 head escarole lettuce, well washed and torn

One 5-oz (150 g) pkg baby spinach, washed

¼ cup chopped pecans (60 mL)

1 pomegranate, seeds only

1 ruby red grapefruit, segmented

1 red onion, thinly sliced

2 Tbsp pomegranate juice (30 mL)

2 Tbsp sherry vinegar (30 mL)

¼ cup grape seed oil (60 mL)

1 tsp honey (5 mL)

1 tsp Dijon mustard (5 mL)

Sea salt and freshly cracked black peppercorns

Combine the greens in a medium bowl. Sprinkle with pecans, pomegranate seeds, grapefruit segments, and onions.

Make the dressing by whisking together pomegranate juice, sherry vinegar, grape seed oil, honey, and Dijon mustard in a small bowl. Adjust the seasoning with salt and pepper to taste. Toss with greens and serve.

< MAKES 6 SERVING >

AUTUMN VEGETABLE SOUP

Soups are a staple for me in the fall and winter, but sometimes I just don't have the hours it takes to simmer and coax out their maximum flavor. With this brightly colored soup, I've introduced a couple of shortcuts to create texture and maximize flavor. The dried wild mushrooms—in this case chanterelles—add a rich flavor and the red lentils melt away to add a creamy texture to this wholesome soup.

PREP TIME • 20 minutes
COOKING TIME • 40 minutes
SEASON • fall

⅓ cup dried chanterelles or porcini mushrooms (75 mL)
2 Tbsp olive oil (30 mL)
2 Tbsp butter (30 mL)
1 large cooking onion, chopped
1 medium carrot, chopped
1 stalk celery
1 leek, white part only, chopped
1 tsp peeled and chopped fresh ginger (5 mL)
2 sprigs fresh thyme
2 broccoli stems, trimmed and sliced into ⅛-inch medallions
2 sweet potatoes, peeled and chopped
1 bay leaf
4 cups chicken or vegetable stock (1 L)
¼ cup red lentils (60 mL)
Sea salt and freshly cracked black peppercorns
1 cup broccoli florets (250 mL)

Soak the mushrooms in hot water for 10 minutes to soften. Remove from water and set aside; discard the liquid.

Meanwhile, in a large pot over medium heat, add the oil and butter and sweat the onions, carrot, celery, leek, ginger, and thyme for about 4 minutes, stirring with a wooden spoon until the onion is translucent.

Add the remaining ingredients, except florets; season and bring to a boil. Cover, reduce heat to low, and cook for 20 to 25 minutes or until the potatoes are tender. Taste for seasoning and adjust if necessary.

Just before serving, bring back to a simmer and add the broccoli florets. Cover and steam for 2 minutes or until just tender and still crunchy. For added flavor, serve the soup drizzled with extra virgin olive oil.

< MAKES 6 SERVINGS >

UDON MUSHROOM NOODLE SOUP

This is a quick way to enjoy the delicious and healthy Japanese noodles you've probably seen in restaurants, at home. There are several key ingredients that can only be purchased at specialty Asian food stores, namely udon noodles, bonito flakes, and kombu seaweed. All the other ingredients can be found at the seafood counter in your local grocery store. The equal volume of tamari soy sauce and mirin—a sweet Japanese rice wine—give the broth its secret balance.

PREP TIME • 15 minutes
COOKING TIME • 20 minutes
SEASON • all seasons

6 cups chicken stock (1.5 L)

1 sheet kombu seaweed

1 oz bonito flakes (25 g)

½ cup dried shiitake mushrooms (125 mL)

⅓ cup tamari soy sauce (75 mL)

⅓ cup mirin (75 mL)

9 oz frozen pre-cooked udon noodles (270 g)

1 sheet toasted seaweed, cut into thin strips with scissors

One 5-oz (150-g) pkg baby spinach, blanched, squeezed of excess liquid, and chopped

One 3½-oz (90-g) pkg enoki mushrooms

Seven-spice mixture or sansho, for garnish, optional

3 scallions, thinly sliced, for garnish

In a pot on medium high, heat the chicken broth with the kombu until it comes to a boil. Reduce heat to very low and gently simmer for 10 minutes (kombu should never boil rapidly; if it does, it will impart a harsh flavor to your soup). Remove from heat and add the bonito flakes. Let stand for 10 minutes to develop the flavor. Strain the broth into a clean pot and discard the bonito and kombu.

Return the liquid to the pot on the stovetop and add the shiitake mushrooms; simmer, uncovered, over low heat for 5 minutes to continue developing the flavor. (If making soup without bonito and kombu, use just the shiitake mushrooms instead and follow the same procedure as above). After 5 minutes, add the tamari soy sauce and mirin; stir (don't discard the shiitake). Add the pre-cooked noodles to the soup and warm gently for 1 minute until heated through.

To serve, place a small handful of enoki mushrooms, toasted seaweed strips, cooked spinach, and scallions into the bottom of 4 bowls. Using tongs, divide the noodles evenly into each bowl and pour the hot broth overtop. Sprinkle with seven-spice mixture or sansho pepper, if desired, and garnish with scallions before serving.

< MAKES 4 TO 6 SERVINGS >

In my mind, part of having fun in the kitchen means avoiding boredom. Fish and seafood lend themselves to such versatile flavor combinations, and there's such a variety to choose from, it's easy to keep things fresh and interesting. Sometimes, when we're just in the mood for a familiar favorite, I'll buy a whole small fish and bake it with tons of herbs and capers, and slather it in olive oil (my Greek upbringing takes over occasionally).

Another part of having fun in the kitchen is enjoying the fruits of my labor. A whole fish is meant to be eaten by hand so, although I do use a knife and fork for the fillet, there are all those leftover bits in the pan to consider. And let's not forget the bones with all that succulent meat still attached! My mother, when eating, can clean a fish like a cat. I don't go that far but there's always a piece of bread involved in sopping up the pan juices.

The most fun, for me, is following the "pure" food philosophy of buying the freshest fish available and imagining how I'm going to cook it. I've devised a plan that ensures I feature fresh seafood at least twice a week: I buy fish on Tuesdays—the day I know my fishmonger gets a fresh batch—and enough for two dinners. You might be thinking, "I thought you had to cook fish the day you bought it?" But, by knowing the day the fish arrives fresh, I give myself some leeway and can safely keep fish that's fresh in my fridge for 2 days. That way we can have fish on Tuesdays and Thursdays. I also keep an open mind when I go into the store and buy whichever fish is freshest, and inspires me.

fish & seafood

PANKO-CRUSTED OYSTERS WITH POMEGRANATE SOY GLAZE

This is an elegant dish to serve when you're entertaining and in the mood for something other than oysters on the half shell. The panko (Japanese breadcrumbs) gives the oysters a tempura-like texture. I love these served in a little Asian spoon or in scallop shells: it makes for an appealing presentation. Because of the summer spawn, the best seasons for oysters are fall or winter, when its texture is less fatty.

PREP TIME • 25 minutes
COOKING TIME • 10 minutes
SEASON • fall/winter

12 oysters, shucked
Freshly cracked black peppercorns
All-purpose flour, for dredging
1 egg, beaten
1 Tbsp water (15 mL)
½ cup panko or regular breadcrumbs (125 mL)
¼ cup vegetable oil, for frying (60 mL)
5 snow peas, julienned
1 tsp sesame oil (5 mL), for frying
Snow pea shoots or pea shoots

Pomegranate Soy Glaze
¼ cup pomegranate juice (60 mL)
2 Tbsp tamari soy sauce (30 mL)
1 Tbsp honey (15 mL)

In a small skillet, combine pomegranate juice, tamari soy sauce, and honey and cook on medium heat until thick and syrupy, about 5 minutes; set aside.

Pat the oysters dry with a paper towel and then season with cracked peppercorns to taste. Place the flour, egg, and panko breadcrumbs in three separate small bowls. Add the water to the egg and whisk to combine. Dredge each oyster in the flour and then dip in the egg wash before pressing both sides into the panko. Transfer the panko-coated oysters to a medium plate.

In a large skillet, heat the vegetable oil over high. Cook the coated oysters for about 1 minute per side or until golden and crisp. Remove to a paper-towel lined plate.

In a small skillet, heat the sesame oil on high. Add the snow peas and toss lightly for about 1 minute or until just heated through. Remove from heat.

To serve, arrange a couple of oysters on each plate or on a serving platter. Sprinkle with the snow pea shoots and drizzle with a small amount of glaze.

< MAKES 4 APPETIZER PORTIONS >

MUSSELS IN SPICY COCONUT TOMATO BROTH

I love cooking mussels for supper! They are versatile, easy to prepare, and they cook in about 10 minutes max. This recipe is perfect for improvising so don't feel married to any of the ingredients. Once you've enjoyed every morsel of the meat, just sop up all that flavorful broth with some crusty, warm bread. All you need is a salad on the side and it's dinner.

PREP TIME • 15 minutes
COOKING TIME • 20 minutes
SEASON • all seasons

2 Tbsp vegetable oil (30 mL)

1 medium sweet onion, sliced

3 cloves garlic, chopped

1 Tbsp grated fresh ginger (15 mL)

1 Thai chili pepper, finely chopped

Grated zest and juice of 1 lime

½ tsp ground coriander seed (2 mL)

½ jar Pure by Christine Cushing Basil Tomato Sauce
    or one 19-oz (540-mL) can plum tomatoes

¼ cup dry sherry (60 mL)

⅔ cup coconut milk (150 mL)

4 lb PEI mussels, bearded and scrubbed well to remove dirt (1.8 kg)

½ bunch fresh Thai basil or cilantro, chopped

Sea salt and freshly cracked black peppercorns

In a large deep skillet, heat the oil on a medium high setting. Add the onion and sauté for about 2 to 3 minutes, stirring often, until just soft. Add the garlic, ginger, chili pepper, rind, and coriander seeds; sauté for about 2 minutes or until the garlic is golden. Add the tomato sauce or tomatoes and simmer, uncovered; continue to cook for about 8 minutes more or until the liquid is slightly reduced.

Add the sherry, coconut milk, lime juice, and mussels and season to taste. Cover and steam over medium heat for 5 to 7 minutes or until the mussels open. Remove from heat immediately, discarding any unopened mussels. Stir in fresh coriander and adjust seasoning before serving.

< MAKES 4 TO 6 SERVINGS >

MOROCCAN SHRIMP

This quick shrimp recipe sings with the contrasting flavors—sweet, spicy, salty, and tart—reminiscent of Moroccan cuisine. The shrimp can be grilled, sautéed, or broiled and served hot or at room temperature. I find it's the perfect "small plate" sharing dish.

PREP TIME • 10 minutes
COOKING TIME • 5 minutes
SEASON • all seasons

½ lb shelled, deveined shrimp (raw, medium), tail on (250 g)
Grated zest of 1 lemon
2 cloves garlic, chopped
¼ tsp ground cinnamon (1 mL)
Splash chipotle Tabasco Sauce
2 Tbsp olive oil (30 mL)
Sea salt
Freshly cracked Szechuan or black peppercorns
Juice of ½ lemon
2 Tbsp fresh chopped cilantro (30 mL)

In a medium bowl, combine the shrimp, lemon zest, garlic, cinnamon, and Tabasco Sauce. Cover and refrigerate for up to 3 hours or until ready to cook.

Heat the oil in a large skillet over high. Add the shrimp mixture and toss rapidly for 2 to 3 minutes, just until shrimp starts to curl. Season with sea salt and pepper. Add the lemon juice and fresh cilantro, and serve immediately in a small platter for sharing.

< MAKES 4 SERVINGS >

SHRIMP AND MUSHROOM STIR-FRY WITH CRUNCHY GINGER

I was absolutely wowed by the combination of flavors in this brightly colored stir-fry when I first made it. Mirin, added at the end, introduces just a hint of sweetness but it's enough to balance the saltiness of the soy. To set the record straight, mirin is a sweet Japanese rice wine, not rice wine vinegar, which has a different flavor. If you can't find mirin, use sake or a tablespoon of granulated sugar.

PREP TIME • 25 minutes
COOKING TIME • 10 minutes
SEASON • all seasons

1-inch-thick slice of peeled fresh ginger
2 Tbsp vegetable oil (30 mL)
12 large shrimp, peeled and deveined, with tail on
Grated zest of 1 orange
½ tsp chili flakes (2 mL)
1 small onion, thinly sliced
1 cup sliced shiitake mushrooms (250 mL)
1 clove garlic, chopped
1 red bell pepper, seeded and cut into strips
1 cup snow peas, trimmed (250 mL)
3 Tbsp tamari soy sauce (45 mL)
1 Tbsp mirin (15 mL)

Slice the ginger into thin medallions and stack them up a few at a time. Slice these stacks into thin julienne strips. Heat the vegetable oil in a wok over high until hot but not smoking. Add the ginger and cook until crisp and golden, about 1 minute. Remove the ginger and set aside.

Add the shrimp, orange zest, and chili flakes to the wok; toss until the shrimp are just opaque, about 2 minutes. Remove the shrimp and set aside.

Add the onion, mushrooms, garlic, and red bell pepper to the wok; toss for about 3 to 4 minutes until the vegetables are soft and golden.

Add the snow peas, the pre-cooked shrimp, tamari soy sauce, and mirin; toss for about 1 minute, just to soften the snow peas. Sprinkle with crunchy ginger and serve immediately over steamed rice.

< MAKES 4 SERVINGS >

WARM SALMON SALAD WITH BALSAMIC GLAZE

I came up with this salad one evening, after I'd just purchased fresh salmon. All I had was fennel and Belgian endive so, I thought, what the heck? It's a great appetizer, or perfect—in a larger portion—for a main course accompanied by basmati pilaf or a vegetable roast.

PREP TIME • 15 minutes
COOKING TIME • 10 minutes
SEASON • all seasons

1 head raw fennel, thinly sliced

1 head radicchio di Treviso or Belgian endive

1 Tbsp balsamic vinegar (15 mL)

2 Tbsp extra virgin olive oil for finishing (30 mL)

Salt and freshly ground black pepper

4 salmon fillets, 1-inch thick, skin on (about 4 oz each) (125 g)

1 Tbsp cracked fennel seeds (15 mL)

½ tsp ground sumac, optional (2 mL)

Sea salt and freshly cracked black peppercorns

1 Tbsp grape seed oil (15 mL)

1 Tbsp balsamic vinegar (15 mL)

In a medium bowl, toss together the fennel, radicchio, balsamic vinegar, olive oil, and salt and pepper to taste. Let stand to wilt slightly while the salmon is cooking.

Meanwhile, in a small bowl, combine the fennel seeds, sumac (if using), sea salt, and pepper; stir to blend. Sprinkle the salmon fillets, on the skinless side, with the spice mixture.

In a large, heavy skillet, heat the grape seed oil on high. (If using a lighter, non-stick skillet, cook on medium heat.) Place the fish fillets in the skillet and sear, skin-side down, for about 3 to 4 minutes or just until the skin starts to crisp. Reduce heat to low.

Remove the skillet from the heat and drain the excess fish fat. Drizzle the fillets with balsamic vinegar and return the skillet to the stovetop. Cover immediately and continue to cook—without flipping—for another 3 to 4 minutes or until the salmon is cooked but still soft in the center. A knife, when inserted into the very middle of the fish, should come out feeling just warm to the touch.

Divide the fennel mixture among four plates and top each with a salmon fillet.

< MAKES 4 SERVINGS >

PAN-ROASTED HALIBUT WITH SHALLOTS AND GRAPE TOMATOES

Every member of my extended family has the same reaction when I mention I'm making pan-roasted halibut: they'll be coming for dinner— it's their favorite. This recipe is so versatile: I can adjust the ingredients to whatever I have in the fridge. I sometimes add sweet peppers or pancetta and substitute limes for lemons.

PREP TIME • 10 minutes
COOKING TIME • 25 minutes
SEASON • summer/fall

4 pieces skinless, boneless halibut, each piece about 6 oz (170 g)
Grated zest and juice of ½ lemon
1 Tbsp chopped fresh thyme (15 mL)
Sea salt and freshly cracked black peppercorns
3 Tbsp extra virgin olive oil (45 mL)
Splash dry white wine or vermouth, optional
1 cup grape tomatoes, cut in half (250 mL)
2 whole shallots, peeled and thinly sliced lengthwise
Lemon wedges and chopped fresh parsley, for garnish

Preheat the oven to 375°F (190°C).

Season the fish with lemon zest, thyme, and salt and pepper to taste. Heat 2 Tbsp olive oil in a large, oven-proof skillet or sauté pan over medium high. Sear the fish for about 1 to 2 minutes per side or until just golden. Remove from heat and transfer the fish to a plate.

Immediately deglaze the pan with a splash of white wine and lemon juice. Add the last tablespoon of olive oil along with the tomatoes, shallots, and salt and pepper to taste. Transfer the pan to the oven and bake for 7 to 10 minutes or just until the onions and tomatoes start to soften.

Remove from the oven and place the fish pieces overtop the tomato mixture. Return the pan to the oven and roast for about 7 to 9 minutes, moving the vegetables in the pan in the middle of the process, until the fish is cooked through and firm. A small knife, when inserted into the middle of the fish, should come out feeling just warm to the touch.

Transfer the fish and vegetables onto four plates. Drizzle each plate with some of the pan juices and garnish with lemon wedges and chopped fresh parsley before serving.

< MAKES 4 SERVINGS >

CRISPY JAMAICAN SNAPPER WITH FRIED PLANTAIN

This dish is a trip to Jamaica on a plate. The fried plantain, which I love, makes for a great accompaniment with this snapper recipe; prepare it first and serve at room temperature. Unlike bananas, plantain is best—creamy and with a sweet texture—when it's almost black on the outside. I've created a pseudo jerk-seasoning mix to rub on this moist and mild fish and a simple coconut sauce, which tastes like a rum daiquiri. Together, the seasoning and sauce make an unusually delicious flavor pairing.

PREP TIME • 15 minutes
COOKING TIME • 10 minutes
SEASON • all seasons

4 sprigs fresh thyme, leaves only, chopped

¼ Scotch bonnet chili pepper, seeded and finely chopped

1 Tbsp finely grated fresh ginger (15 mL)

¼ tsp ground allspice (1 mL)

2 Tbsp butter, for frying (30 mL)

1 very ripe plantain, peeled, sliced into rounds ¼-inch thick

Vegetable oil

4 pieces red snapper fillet, trout or catfish (about 6 oz/175 g each)

Sea salt

Rum Coconut Sauce

½ cup coconut milk (125 mL)

¼ cup (60 mL) canned pumpkin purée (freeze remainder for pie)

2 Tbsp dark rum (30 mL)

1 tsp freshly squeezed lime juice (5 mL)

In a small bowl, combine the thyme, chili pepper, ginger, and allspice. Season both sides of the fillets with salt and, using a sharp knife, score the skin side of each three times. Rub the fish with the spice mixture on all sides.

In a small frying pan, fry the plantain slices in 1 inch of vegetable oil over medium heat, 3 minutes per side; set aside on paper towels.

In a medium saucepan, combine the coconut milk, pumpkin purée, rum, and lime juice. Season with salt and pepper and bring to a boil over medium heat. Reduce heat to low and simmer, uncovered, for 5 minutes or until thick and creamy. Set aside.

In a large, nonstick skillet, melt the butter over medium heat. Pan-fry the fillets, skin-side down, for 3 to 4 minutes or until crisp. Flip the fillets carefully and fry the other side about 3 minutes or until the fish is firm and cooked through. If the pan is too crowded, fry 2 fillets at a time. Transfer the pan-fried fillets to a platter, drizzle with sauce, and serve with lime wedges and the fried plantain.

< MAKES 4 SERVINGS >

INDIAN-SPICED TROUT

I've been predicting that the Indian spice route would eventually make its way to our kitchens for several years now. I think it's finally starting to happen and this recipe will further your love of cooking simple Indian at home. There are a number of great quality spice blends (also known as "masala") that can be purchased in grocery stores and that will make this trout really flavorful. Old jars of curry powder have a very stale flavor and just won't cut it here.

PREP TIME • 20 minutes
COOKING TIME • 15 minutes
SEASON • all seasons

4 rainbow trout fillets, about 5 to 6 oz each (150 to 75 g)

1 tsp toasted cumin seeds (5 mL)

½ tsp crushed dry chili pepper (2 mL)

1 large clove garlic, minced

1 Tbsp grated fresh ginger (15 mL)

1 Tbsp good quality curry masala (15 mL)

Pinch ground cardamom

1 Tbsp freshly squeezed lime juice (15 mL)

Sea salt and freshly cracked black peppercorns

¼ cup clarified butter or vegetable oil, for brushing (60 mL)

Cilantro sprigs and lime wedges, for garnish

Preheat the oven to 400°F (200°C).

Grind the cumin in a mortar and pestle or in a spice grinder. Transfer to a bowl and stir in the crushed chili pepper, minced garlic, ginger, curry masala, cardamom, lemon juice, and 1 Tbsp of clarified butter or vegetable oil just to soften the mixture.

Brush both sides of the trout with clarified butter or vegetable oil and season with salt. Rub the spice blend on the flesh side of the fish to coat well. Put the fillets, skin-side down, on a parchment lined baking sheet and bake approximately 14 to 16 minutes until the fish is firm to the touch and cooked through.

Garnish with cilantro sprigs and lime wedges. Serve with a pilaf and Yogurt Drizzle (see p. 100).

< MAKES 4 SERVINGS >

BLACK COD IN CRAZY WATER

This fun recipe is a twist on a classic Italian spicy broth called "Aqua Pazza." Here I use an unusual combination—for fish—of red wine and wild mushrooms. If black cod is unavailable, substitute with a rich fish such as salmon or arctic char, which can handle the spice and red wine.

PREP TIME • 15 minutes
COOKING TIME • 20 minutes
SEASON • all seasons

1½ lb black cod fillet, skin on and sliced into 4 pieces (750 g) about 2 inches (5 cm) thick and 6 oz (175 g) each

Sea salt and freshly cracked black peppercorns

8 round, very thin slices of pancetta

2 sprigs fresh tarragon

1½ Tbsp olive oil (22 mL)

2 shallots, sliced

2 cloves garlic, sliced

1 dried chili pepper, crushed

½ cup dry medium body red wine (125 mL)

1 cup fish stock or clam juice (250 mL)

1 Tbsp dried porcini mushrooms, soaked in hot water for 5 minutes (15 mL)

1 Tbsp tomato paste (15 mL)

Extra virgin olive oil for drizzling

Chopped fresh tarragon leaves, for garnish

Preheat the oven to 375°F (190°C).

Season the flesh side of the cod. Place, skin-side down, on a plate. Top each piece of cod with half a sprig of tarragon, broken up, and with 2 rounds of slightly overlapping pancetta.

In a large, deep skillet, heat the oil on medium high. Sear the pancetta-covered side for about 4 minutes or until golden. Transfer the seared fish, skin-side down, onto a parchment paper-lined medium baking dish. Place in the oven and bake for about 12 to 14 minutes or until the fish is firm and cooked through.

Drain the excess fat from the skillet and return to medium-high heat. Sauté the shallots in the skillet for 2 minutes or until soft. Add the garlic and chili pepper. Reduce heat to medium and continue to sauté until the garlic is just golden. Deglaze with red wine and stock or clam juice. Add the drained porcini mushrooms and tomato paste. Whisk and simmer, uncovered, for 8 to 10 minutes or until the sauce is reduced by half.

Place the baked fish into shallow bowls. Pour broth over each and then drizzle with extra virgin olive oil. Sprinkle with tarragon and serve immediately.

< MAKES 4 SERVINGS >

BAKED BRANZINI WITH CHARD AND CAPERS

This Mediterranean-style recipe is such a low-maintenance dish it's a great opportunity to try a new fish on your menu. Try spigola, porgy, or snapper, to name a few. Feel free to use fillets if you don't like bones and change the herbs and veggies. If you want soft veggies, cook for 15 minutes before adding the fillets. Removing the fillets of a cooked whole fish can be a bit messy, but it just takes a bit of practice. While the fish is baking, you can whip up a salad or rice dish and dinner is ready.

PREP TIME • 15 minutes
COOKING TIME • 40 minutes
SEASON • all seasons

2 whole branzini or spigola (about 1½ lb/750 g each)

3 Tbsp extra virgin olive oil (45 mL)

Sea salt and freshly cracked black peppercorns

½ red onion, thinly sliced

½ bunch Swiss chard, sliced

2 cloves garlic, thinly sliced

2 bay leaves

½ cup white wine (125 mL)

½ tsp dried Greek oregano (2 mL)

1 Tbsp capers (15 mL)

1 sprig fresh rosemary, leaves only

1 lemon, thinly sliced into rounds

Preheat the oven to 400°F (200°C).

Drizzle a large rectangular baking dish (about 13 inches long) with 1 Tbsp olive oil and top with the onion slices, Swiss chard, garlic, bay leaves, and white wine. Season the fish's cavity and exterior with plenty of salt and pepper to taste. Place the seasoned fish overtop the other vegetables in the baking dish, leaving some room between each fish. Sprinkle with oregano, capers, and rosemary leaves, and drizzle with the remaining olive oil. Arrange the lemon slices on top of each fish.

Place in the oven and bake, uncovered, for 35 to 40 minutes or until the fish is just cooked through. A good test is to insert a small knife for several seconds into the back of the fish, parallel to the bones. Remove and if the knife is warm to the touch, then the fish is cooked through.

Remove the baking dish from the oven and let cool slightly. Using a spatula, lift the whole fish from the dish and transfer to a platter. Run a knife vertically along the middle of each fish and remove the fillets. Serve with the baked vegetables and drippings from the pan.

< MAKES 4 TO 6 SERVINGS >

WEEKNIGHT SEAFOOD PAELLA

Here's a way to enjoy the flavors of pæella in a fraction of the time. To prevent having a sandy pæella, make sure you immerse the clams in large bowls of cold water while scrubbing. Repeat the process several times and add some salt to the last batch. The clams will think they are in the ocean and spit out a little of the sand trapped inside. It's a cool trick.

PREP TIME • 25 minutes
COOKING TIME • 20 minutes
SEASON • all seasons

1 ¾ cups water (425 mL)

2 Tbsp olive oil (30 mL)

Sea salt and freshly cracked black peppercorns

1 cup good quality long grain rice (250 mL)

¼ cup extra virgin olive oil (60 mL)

1 large onion, chopped

1 leek, white part only, sliced

2 large cloves garlic, chopped

1 bay leaf

¼ tsp saffron threads (1 mL)

Juice of 1 lemon

1 cup dry white wine (250 mL)

8 medium clams, scrubbed and well washed

16 medium mussels, scrubbed and bearded

16 large shrimp, peeled and deveined, tail on

Several sprigs flat-leaf parsley, chopped, for garnish

In a medium pot, bring the water, oil, salt, and pepper to a boil. Add the rice, reduce heat to a simmer, stir, and cover; cook for about 20 minutes or until the rice is tender. Remove the pot from the heat and let stand, covered, for about 5 minutes. Spread the rice onto a large serving platter and set aside to cool.

In a large pot, heat the oil on high. Add the onion, leek, garlic, bay leaf, and saffron. Sauté for about 3 minutes or until the onion begins to soften. Add the wine and lemon juice and bring to a boil. Add the clams and reduce heat to medium. Cover and simmer for about 5 minutes; the clam shells should still be closed. Add the mussels and shrimp and continue simmering, covered, for another 4 minutes. If the mussels and clams haven't opened, remove the shrimp and continue cooking until the shells open. Remove from the heat and season with cracked black peppercorns.

Pour the warm seafood mixture, including the juices, overtop the rice. Sprinkle with lots of chopped flat-leaf parsley and serve warm or at room temperature.

< MAKES 4 SERVINGS >

In my kitchen, I cook chicken a couple of times a week, on average. In the summer, that means a lot of drumsticks or thighs on the grill. (You'll notice I didn't mention chicken breasts on the grill—that's because I think they're best cooked whole on the bird or in a stir-fry, which keeps them moist.) I've also equipped my barbecue with a rotisserie for roasting a whole bird. I get so excited watching that chicken slowly twirl round and round, basting itself. I keep opening the lid to make sure it's still there.

In the cooler months, I love the crispy golden-roasted chicken in the oven, surrounded by lots of seasonal veggies.

At some point, I got into this great habit of keeping the chicken carcass with leftover wings or thighs attached to make a pasta sauce the next day. Can I tell you how much flavor those roasted bones and drippings add to a sauce! All I do is break apart the bones and cover the whole lot with water—drippings included. I bring it to a boil and let simmer for 30 minutes, then pull apart the meat and strain out the bones. This sauce can be added to any of the pasta recipes in this book for a boost of flavor, or use it in place of chicken stock.

poultry

NIÇOISE CHICKEN

This is a familiar and soothing southern French-inspired dish that combines a ratatouille—bell peppers and zucchini—and a quick-braised chicken in a rich tomato sauce with a splash of brandy. If you can find them, use small, black niçoise olives, which will give the chicken a little salty hit.

PREP TIME • 20 minutes
COOKING TIME • 30 minutes
SEASON • all seasons

1 small zucchini, cut into ½ inch dice
½ red bell pepper, cut into ½ inch dice
1 small Italian eggplant, cut into ½ inch dice
2 sprigs fresh thyme
3 Tbsp olive oil (45 mL)
8 boneless, skinless chicken thighs
2 small cloves garlic, chopped
1 tsp Greek oregano (5 mL)
3 Tbsp brandy (45 mL)
1 cup Pure by Christine Cushing Basil Tomato Sauce
        or 1 small 19-oz (540-mL) can plum tomatoes
½ cup water (125 mL)
Chopped fresh basil, for garnish
¼ cup (60 mL) niçoise olives or Italian-style small olives
Sea salt and freshly cracked black peppercorns

Preheat the oven to 400°F (200°C).

Line a large baking sheet with parchment paper. Spread the zucchini, bell pepper, and egg-plant onto the sheet and drizzle with 2 Tbsp olive oil. Season with salt and pepper to taste and toss on the sprigs of thyme. Stir to coat the veggies with oil. Roast in the oven for 18 to 20 minutes or until golden and evenly cooked. Remove from the oven and set aside.

While the vegetables are roasting, brown the chicken in 1 Tbsp of olive oil in a large sauce-pan over medium high for 4 minutes or until golden. Reduce the heat to medium, add the garlic and oregano and cook—stirring often—for 2 more minutes just to soften the garlic. Deglaze with the brandy. Cover and cook for 4 more minutes. If the meat sticks to the pan, add a splash of water to loosen. Season with salt and pepper to taste before adding the tomato sauce and water.

Reduce the heat to medium low and simmer, covered, for 5 minutes. Add the roasted vegetables and continue to simmer, covered, for 5 more minutes to thicken the sauce and fully cook the chicken.

Add the olives and chopped basil, adjust the seasoning, and serve with fresh bread or rice.

< MAKES 4 SERVINGS >

SHERRY-SPIKED GRILLED QUAIL

Quail is readily available these days at your specialty meat counter, close to where you'll find duck meat. I cook quail on medium heat, which prevents it from drying out and keeps the skin from being scorched before the meat is cooked. I never leave my quail unattended while grilling for this reason. This recipe for grilled quail makes a delicious appetizer for a get-together with friends. Besides, food is so much more fun when you eat it with your hands.

PREP TIME • 50 minutes
COOKING TIME • 10 minutes
SEASON • summer/fall

4 whole quail

Marinade

2 Tbsp tamari soy sauce (30 mL)
1 tsp fresh grated ginger (5 mL)
2 cloves garlic, finely minced
Juice and grated zest of 1 lime
Juice and grated zest of 1 orange
2 Tbsp sherry (30 mL)
⅓ bunch chopped fresh mint
2 scallions, finely minced
2 Tbsp maple syrup (30 mL)
Sea salt and freshly cracked black peppercorns

Slice the quail in half lengthwise, removing the backbone with a cleaver or heavy shears. (You can ask your butcher to do this or buy the quail already cut in half.)

In a medium bowl, combine all the marinade ingredients except the oil, sea salt, and pepper; stir well. Add the quail to the marinade and toss to coat well. Cover and chill in the fridge for 30 minutes or for as long as 2 hours.

Preheat the grill to medium high. Remove the marinated quail from the fridge and season with salt and pepper to taste.

Grill the quail until crisp and evenly browned on all sides but still pink inside, about 3 to 4 minutes per side: the quail will quickly dry out if it's well done. (As an alternative, sear the quail in a hot skillet with 1 Tbsp vegetable oil for 1 to 2 minutes per side before transferring to a 375°F/190°C oven for about 3 to 4 minutes or until just pink in the middle.) Serve immediately as an appetizer.

< MAKES 4 SERVINGS >

TARRAGON CHICKEN BREAST WITH PARMESAN TUILE (see image on p. 77)

This is one of the few ways I like to cook chicken breast. By cooking it "restaurant style" (beginning on the stove-top and finishing in the oven), the skin is nice and crisp and the meat is tender and juicy. Baking chicken with its skin on keeps the meat moist. However, if you want to reduce the fat, swap Dijon mustard for butter and remove the skin once it's cooked.

PREP TIME • 15 minutes
COOKING TIME • 25 minutes
SEASON • all seasons

¾ cup coarsely grated Parmesan cheese (175 mL)

4 sprigs fresh thyme, leaves only, chopped

4 medium chicken breasts, boneless, skin on,
    each about 6 to 7 oz (175 to 200 g)

2 Tbsp butter, at room temperature (30 mL)

2 tsp chopped tarragon (10 mL)

Sea salt and freshly cracked black peppercorns

1 Tbsp grape seed oil (15 mL)

1 Tbsp sherry vinegar (15 mL)

¼ cup dry vermouth wine (60 mL)

½ cup chicken stock (125 mL)

1 Tbsp cold butter (15 mL)

1 tsp chopped fresh tarragon (5 mL)

Fresh tarragon sprigs for garnish

Preheat the oven to 400°F (200°C).

In a small bowl, add the Parmesan and thyme and hand toss to blend. Divide the cheese mixture into four equal piles, each about 3 inches in diameter, on a parchment paper-lined baking sheet. Make sure to leave at least a 2-inch space between each mound. Bake in the oven for about 10 minutes or until the Parmesan tuiles are golden and crisp. Remove from the oven and set aside.

Meanwhile, in a small bowl and using a fork, mash 2 Tbsp soft butter with 2 tsp tarragon. Loosen the skin of the chicken breasts by carefully sliding your fingers underneath. Smear ¼ of the butter mixture under the skin of each breast, pressing down to distribute evenly.

Season the outside of the chicken with salt and pepper to taste. Heat the oil in a large, ovenproof sauté pan over high until hot but not smoking. Add the chicken and sear, skin-side down, for about 4 minutes or until golden. Shake the pan once or twice to keep the skin from sticking. Put the pan in the oven and cook for 4 minutes. Flip the breasts over and continue cooking in the oven for about 4 to 5 minutes or until the meat is firm and the juices run clear. Remove the chicken to a large plate and tent with foil to keep warm.

Discard the fat from the sauté pan. Return the pan to the stovetop and deglaze with sherry vinegar over medium high. Add the vermouth and stock and continue cooking for another 3 to 5 minutes: the liquid should still be runny, not thick, but slightly reduced. Swirl in the remaining tablespoon of butter. Add the chopped tarragon and adjust the seasoning.

Place the chicken on four plates. Pour the sauce overtop and garnish with tarragon sprigs and one Parmesan tuile each before serving.

< MAKES 4 SERVINGS >

MEXICAN-SPICED CHICKEN DRUMSTICKS

These golden beauties feature the smoky notes of chipotle chili peppers with just a touch of sweetness. I'm hooked on moist dark meat, as you'll see from the other recipes in this chapter, but you can use these flavors on a chicken breast, if you prefer.

PREP TIME • 10 minutes
COOKING TIME • 35 minutes
SEASON • all seasons

12 chicken drumsticks
2 Tbsp olive oil (30 mL)
2 cloves garlic, finely chopped
½ chipotle chili pepper canned, chopped
1 tsp cumin seed, toasted and ground (5 mL)
Juice and zest of 1 lime
1 Tbsp smoked paprika (15 mL)
1 Tbsp brown sugar (15 mL)
Sea salt and freshly cracked black peppercorns
½ bunch chopped fresh parsley, for garnish

Preheat the oven to 400°F (200°C).

Combine the drumsticks with all the ingredients in a large bowl, except the parsley; toss to coat well.

Arrange in a single layer in a small roasting pan. Bake for about 30 to 35 minutes, flipping over half way through until the chicken is cooked and golden brown. Sprinkle with parsley and serve.

< MAKES 4 TO 6 SERVINGS >

BLACK BEAN CHICKEN WITH GAI-LAN

Stir-fries are a great way to get everything—except the rice—into one pot. Because all the ingredients cook so quickly, I always recommend chopping in advance before firing up the wok. Gai-lan, also known as Chinese broccoli or Chinese kale, is a hearty Asian leaf vegetable that I love ordering when I eat out, so I figured, "Why not master it at home?" This recipe is the result! (For more on gai-lan, see the introduction on p. 22.)

PREP TIME • 15 minutes
COOKING TIME • 10 minutes
SEASON • all seasons

4 stems gai-lan, peeled
2 Tbsp vegetable oil (30 mL)
2 medium chicken breasts (both should total about 1 lb/500 g),
     cut into ½ inch slices
1 tsp grated fresh ginger (5 mL)
1 small onion, sliced
3 cloves garlic, sliced
1 yellow bell pepper, sliced
¼ tsp dried chili flakes (1 mL)
2 Tbsp black bean sauce (30 mL)
3 Tbsp tamari soy sauce (45 mL)
¼ cup chicken stock (60 mL)

Trim the bottom of the gai-lan stems and peel about 2 inches of the tough, dark-green skin. Cut the trimmed and partially peeled stems into 2-inch long pieces. Keep the leaves whole.

In a medium pot, blanch the gai-lan leaves and stem in boiling salted water for 2 to 3 minutes or until just tender. Drain and set aside.

In a wok, heat the oil on high until hot but not smoking. Add the chicken and ginger and toss for 2 minutes or until the chicken is just golden. Add the onion and toss for 1 more minute to soften. Add the garlic, bell pepper, and chili flakes; toss quickly until the pepper is just tender, about 2 minutes. Add the bean sauce, tamari soy sauce, chicken stock, and the blanched gai-lan.

Stir-fry quickly for 1 minute to combine the ingredients and cook the chicken. Serve immediately over a bed of rice.

< MAKES 4 SERVINGS >

CHIPOTLE COCONUT CHICKEN STICKS WITH TAMARILLO SALSA

You may have noticed the tamarillo, an egg-shaped and deep-orange fruit in the produce aisles. Hailing from South America, the tamarillo is a delicious relative of the tomato with a tart robust flavor that is ideal in this salsa.

PREP TIME • 25 minutes
COOKING TIME • 20 minutes
SEASON • summer/fall

8 wooden skewers, soaked in water for ½ an hour.
2 boneless and skinless chicken breasts, about 1 lb (500 g)
    total weight, cut into ½-inch-thick strips
¼ cup grape seed oil (60 mL)
½ bunch green onions, chopped
1 tsp chopped chipotle, canned (5 mL)
1 clove garlic, smashed
Juice of ½ lime
½ tsp ground coriander seed (2 mL)

Salsa
1 kiwi, peeled and finely diced
Juice of ½ lime
1 tamarillo, peeled and finely diced
½ small red onion, finely diced
1 tsp honey (5 mL)

Sea salt
1 egg whisked together with 1 Tbsp (15 mL) water
1 cup unsweetened flaked coconut (250 mL)

Preheat the oven to 375°F (190°C).

While the skewers are soaking in water, in a food processor, combine the oil, green onions, chili pepper, garlic, lime, and coriander seeds; pulse until very smooth. Transfer the mixture to a small bowl and toss with the chicken strips to coat well. Cover and refrigerate for 30 minutes.

In a small bowl, add the kiwi, lime juice, tamarillo, onion, honey, salt, and coconut; stir until blended. Cover and set aside until ready to use.

Season the chicken with salt and thread onto skewers. Dip into the egg mixture and then roll and press the coconut flakes onto the chicken until fully encrusted. Transfer to a baking tray lined with parchment paper and bake for about 20 minutes, without turning, until the coconut is golden and the chicken is cooked through. Serve with tamarillo salsa, and with the chicken breasts' golden-side up.

< MAKES 4 SERVINGS >

SUMAC-ROASTED CHICKEN WITH CIPOLLINI ONIONS

Throughout the fall and winter my kitchen is filled with the warm smells of crispy, roasted chicken. Sumac, a dark ruby berry indigenous to Italy and the Middle East, is one ingredient that adds a distinctly tangy zip and a great crimson color. Sold ground, in little bags at specialty Middle Eastern stores, its tart flavor is more like that of a sour candy than a lemon. You can always use a lime or lemon as a substitute for ground sumac.

PREP TIME • 10 minutes
COOKING TIME • 60 minutes
SEASON • fall/winter

One 2½-lb (1.2-kg) grain-fed chicken
Sea salt and freshly cracked black peppercorns
½ lemon, quartered
Juice of ½ lemon
1 bay leaf
¼ cup extra virgin olive oil (60 mL)
1 Tbsp Greek oregano (15 mL)
1 tsp Worcestershire sauce (5mL)
1 tsp sea salt (5 mL)
2 tsp ground sumac (10 mL)
½ lb cipollini onions, blanched and peeled,
    or pearl onions (250 g)
1 carrot, peeled and cut into 2-inch sticks
4 medium red potatoes, scrubbed and quartered

Preheat the oven to 400°F (200°C).

Pat the chicken dry and season the cavity generously with half the salt and pepper. Fill the cavity with the lemon and bay leaf. Truss the bird and rub all over the skin with half the olive oil, juice of ½ lemon, and Worcestershire sauce; sprinkle with the oregano, sumac, and sea salt and pepper to taste.

Place the bird in the roasting pan. Arrange the onions, potatoes, and carrots around the chicken and drizzle with the rest of the oil. Season the vegetables and roast in the oven for 55 to 65 minutes or until the juices run clear and the internal temperature of the thigh is 180°F (85°C). If the skin is getting too dark but the chicken still isn't cooked, reduce the oven temperature to 350°F (180°C) for the last fifteen minutes of roasting.

Let rest for 5 minutes before carving.

< MAKES 4 SERVINGS >

TURKEY PAILLARD WITH CREMINI MUSHROOMS

"Paillard" is just a fancy French word for cutlet but it sounds way better. The timing on this dish is essential for best results, but it's also insanely quick. I chop everything first and, while the sauce is reducing, pop the turkey in the oven: by the time the sauce is done, so is the turkey.

PREP TIME • 15 minutes
COOKING TIME • 15 minutes
SEASON • fall/winter

POULTRY

89

Four ¼-inch-thick turkey breast scaloppini (4 oz each/125 g)

Sea salt and freshly cracked black peppercorns

1 tsp chopped fresh sage (5 mL)

All-purpose flour, for dredging

2 Tbsp butter (30 mL)

1 Tbsp grape seed oil (15 mL)

2 tsp Worcestershire sauce (10 mL)

1 shallot, finely chopped

⅓ cup dry vermouth (75 mL)

4 cremini mushrooms, thinly sliced

¾ cup chicken stock (175 mL)

3 whole prunes, pitted and finely chopped

1 tsp Dijon mustard (5 mL)

Fresh sage leaves, for garnish

Preheat the oven to 350°F (180°C).

Season the turkey with salt and pepper and rub with chopped sage. Lightly dredge both sides of the turkey in a shallow bowl of flour.

In a large skillet, over high heat, melt half the butter and grape seed oil. Pan-fry the turkey slices until golden, about 1 minute. Flip the slices and repeat on the other side. Drizzle with Worcestershire sauce. Remove from heat and transfer the turkey to a baking sheet until ready to bake.

In the same skillet, on high, sauté the shallots until soft, about 1 minute. Deglaze with vermouth and add the cremini mushrooms; cook for 2 minutes or until the mushrooms are golden. Reduce heat to medium high, add the stock and prunes, and simmer, uncovered, for 5 to 7 minutes until the liquid is reduced by one third.

Meanwhile, bake the turkey until the meat is no longer pink, about 3 to 4 minutes. Remove immediately or the turkey will dry out. Tent loosely with foil and set aside.

To finish the mushroom sauce, add the last tablespoon butter and Dijon mustard and swirl the pan to thicken slightly; season with salt and pepper to taste. Pour over the reserved turkey, garnish with fresh sage, and serve.

< MAKES 4 SERVINGS >

GREEN TEA-DUSTED DUCK BREAST

Serve this recipe for dinner when you really want to flex your culinary muscle. Using a meat thermometer will ensure you get the internal temperature just right. The Muscovy breed of duck has less fat and more meat on the breast.

PREP TIME • 15 minutes
COOKING TIME • 35 minutes
SEASON • fall/winter

1 to 2 Tbsp ground green tea leaves, about 1 tea bag (15 to 30 mL)
1 tsp ground Szechuan or black peppercorns (5 mL)
¼ tsp ground cloves (1 mL)
1 Tbsp freshly grated ginger (15 mL)
Grated zest of 1 blood orange or regular orange
2 single muscovy duck breasts (each about 1 lb/500 g)
Sea salt

Glaze
2 Tbsp tamari soy sauce (30 mL)
½ cup freshly squeezed blood orange juice (125 mL)
2 Tbsp black currant jam or jelly (30 mL)
½ tsp green tea leaves (2 mL)

Preheat the oven to 350°F (180°C)

Combine tea leaves, pepper, cloves, grated ginger, and orange zest in a small bowl; stir to blend.

Using a sharp knife, score the duck breasts on the fatty side in a criss-cross pattern. Season the breast with sea salt and rub with the tea mixture.

Place the duck, fat-side down, in an ovenproof pan over medium-low heat and render the fat for 3 to 5 minutes. For a mallard duck it might take up to 15 minutes. Remove the duck and drain. (Discard the fat.) The skin should be golden at this point. Flip the breasts and brown the other side for 1 to 2 minutes.

Transfer the pan to the oven and roast, fat-side down, for 4 minutes. Turn the duck breasts over and roast for another 14 to 18 minutes or until the meat has reached an internal temperature of 140°F (60°C) for medium rare. Transfer the duck to a cutting board, tent with aluminium foil, and let rest for 5 minutes. Use a meat thermometer to insure it's at the proper temperature: the duck will be too dry if served above a temperature of 150°F (65°C).

To make the glaze, combine the soy sauce, orange juice, and current jam or jelly in a small saucepan over medium heat. Simmer, uncovered, for about 5 to 7 minutes or until the liquid has the consistency of honey. Add the tea leaves and bring to a boil before removing from the heat.

Thinly slice the duck. Fan out the slices on a platter, drizzle with the warm glaze, and serve immediately.

< MAKES 4 SERVINGS >

Meat night in our house is always a celebration, partly because I try to keep our red meat consumption to a couple of times a week. So, whenever there's the slightest chance that meat's going to hit the grill, there's joy in the air. It's true that the best way to a man's heart is not only through his stomach, but more specifically, through a big fat juicy steak.

Our friends generally share that same enthusiasm, so we can make any night an instant party by just adding meat. We'll spend a little more attention on the wines we pick and probably go easy on the starchy dishes, but not the bread! Meat night is usually accompanied by many green dishes and several varieties of crusty bread.

When we get the mid-afternoon "do you want to get together tonight" phone call, that's another excuse to throw some quick-cooking meat on the grill and to grill everything else alongside it. In fact it has to be pretty darn cold to prevent us from firing up the gas or charcoal barbecue any time of the year.

meat

DECONSTRUCTED BEEF WELLINGTON (see image on p. 93)

I've recently been on a deconstructing binge in which I take apart a traditional dish and reassemble the elements in a different way. It's a fun way to keep inspired. With this Beef Wellington, I've replaced the rolled, pastry-wrapped whole tenderloin with little phyllo pillows that house the mushroom and herb mixture. The crisp phyllo pastry gives it crunch. I've simplified the sauce by adding a little red wine to the pan drippings along with some shallots. Feel free to omit the pastry and just sauté some mushrooms to make it a little quicker.

PREP TIME • 25 minutes
COOKING TIME • 35 minutes
SEASON • all seasons

2 lb center-cut piece of beef tenderloin (1 kg)
1 Tbsp Dijon mustard (15 mL)
1 sprig fresh rosemary, finely chopped
Sea salt and freshly cracked black peppercorns
2 tsp vegetable oil (10 mL)

Sauce
2 Tbsp Butter (30 mL)
2 shallots, finely sliced
½ cup red Burgundy wine (125 mL)
 (other dry red can be substituted)
1 bay leaf

Mushroom Pillows
1 Tbsp butter (15 mL)
1 shallot, finely diced
2 medium-sized king oyster mushrooms, diced
1 fresh sprig tarragon, chopped
Several fresh sprigs chervil, chopped
2 sheets phyllo, cut into 3 strips and wrapped
 in damp towel to prevent drying
Melted butter, for brushing

Preheat the oven to 375°F (190°C).

Rub the meat with Dijon mustard, coating evenly. Sprinkle with rosemary, and sea salt and pepper to taste.

Heat the oil in a medium skillet on medium high. Add the beef and sear for about 4 to 5 minutes, turning often to brown all sides. Transfer the beef to a small roasting pan and roast for about 25 to 27 minutes or until it reaches an internal temperature of 140°F (60°C) for medium rare, or until done to your liking.

Meanwhile, using the same skillet that the beef was seared in, heat the butter on medium.

Add the shallots and sauté, stirring frequently, for about 3 minutes or until very soft and golden. Deglaze with red wine and add the bay leaf. Continue cooking, uncovered, for about 7 to 9 minutes until the liquid is reduced by one third.

Pillows: In a medium skillet, melt the butter and sauté the shallot with the mushrooms and tarragon for about 4 to 5 minutes or until golden. Add the chervil and season with salt and pepper to taste. Remove from the heat and let cool slightly.

Brush 1 side of 2 phyllo sheets with melted butter; position one sheet on top of the other. Spoon one-third of the mushroom mixture on top and in the center of the layered-phyllo square. Fold the bottom and top over—as if you were folding a letter—to completely cover the mushroom filling. Tuck the sides under, about 2 inches on either side, to create a square. Brush the top of the square with melted butter. Repeat with the remaining phyllo sheets, creating a total of 3 mushroom-filled phyllo squares or pillows.

Transfer the phyllo pillows to a small baking sheet and bake in the oven for 10 to 15 minutes until the pastry is golden and puffed.

To serve, slice the tenderloin and place one on each of 6 plates. With a serrated knife, use a sawing motion to cut each mushroom pillow in half. Place one half on top of each tenderloin. Drizzle with the pan juices and garnish with fresh chervil or tarragon sprigs before serving.

< MAKES 6 SERVINGS >

PAPRIKA PORK MEDALLIONS

These juicy little medallions are a great way to serve pork with a classic Spanish combination: sherry and paprika. Medallions cook very quickly and are a testament to how moist and simple pork tenderloin can be. Because this recipe is ready in no time, I usually first prepare a side dish, like green beans with crispy shallots.

PREP TIME • 10 minutes
COOKING TIME • 10 minutes
SEASON • all seasons

2 pork tenderloins, sliced ¼ inch thick on the bias
    (each slice about 1 oz/25 g)
Sea salt and freshly cracked black peppercorns
Flour, for dredging
2 Tbsp olive oil (30 mL)
1 large clove garlic, thinly sliced
⅓ cup dry sherry (75 mL)
½ cup chicken stock (125 mL)
1 tsp sweet paprika (5 mL)
2 Tbsp sour cream (30 mL)
Chopped fresh flat-leaf parsley

Dredge the pork slices lightly in flour and then season with salt and pepper to taste.

Heat the olive oil in a large skillet on medium high. Fry the pork slices, cooking 3 to 4 pieces at a time depending on the size of the pan. Fry for 2 minutes per side until just golden and still slightly pink in the center. Remove the pork from the pan and transfer to a plate; tent with foil. Repeat the process until all the pork slices are cooked, adding more olive oil to the pan if necessary.

Using the same skillet, cook the garlic over medium heat for 1 minute or until just golden, stirring frequently. Add the sherry, paprika, and chicken stock. Reduce for 3 to 4 minutes just to develop the flavor and reduce by half. Remove from the heat and whisk in the sour cream.

Return the pork medallions to the skillet and continue cooking on low for about 1 minute or until the meat is just cooked through. Sprinkle with chopped parsley and serve.

< MAKES 4 SERVINGS >

HERBES DE PROVENCE-CRUSTED LAMB CHOPS

This recipe couldn't be easier and features one of my favorite herb blends: herbes de Provence. The blend of herbs, always sold in a dried form, may vary but most will likely contain rosemary, thyme, and lavender, among other herbs. The aromatic herbes de Provence, perfect for lamb, always transports me back to Provence, where I first tasted it.

PREP TIME • 10 minutes
COOKING TIME • 10 minutes
SEASON • all seasons

12 lamb loin chops (each about 3 oz/75 g)
2 Tbsp olive oil (30 mL)
Sea salt and freshly cracked black peppercorns
2 Tbsp Dijon mustard (30 mL)
¼ cup chopped fresh mint (60 mL)
1 Tbsp herbes de Provence (15 mL)

Preheat the oven to 375°F (190°C).

Season the lamb with salt and pepper; brush both sides with olive oil and rub with Dijon mustard. Use a pastry brush to evenly distribute. Sprinkle both sides with chopped mint and herbes de Provence. Arrange the lamb on a baking sheet and bake for about 12 minutes for medium rare, until still soft but slightly springy to the touch or until done to your liking.

Serve with potatoes, green beans, or sautéed rapini.

< MAKES 4 SERVINGS (3 CHOPS PER PERSON) >

HERBED MEATBALLS WITH GINGER YOGURT DRIZZLE

PREP TIME • 30 minutes
COOKING TIME • 15 minutes
SEASON • all seasons

Meatballs can be made many different ways and using many different ingredients. My family's juicy meatballs are made with tons of herbs and grated onion, which adds moisture. Use lean beef and replace some of that missing animal fat with olive oil, a much healthier fat. If you want to prepare the mixture in advance, leave the salt out until you're ready to cook. These meatballs can be baked in the oven; however, if they are, they won't have the same crispy shell. Serve as part of a meal or as cocktail appetizers.

Several fresh sprigs of mint, leaves only
½ small bunch flat-leaf parsley, leaves only
1 small onion, grated
¼ tsp cumin seeds, toasted and ground (1 mL)
3 Tbsp extra virgin olive oil (45 mL)
1 egg
1 tsp Worcestershire sauce (5 mL)
1 tsp tomato paste (5 mL)
1 lb lean ground beef, preferably chuck (500 g)
1 slice stale whole-grain bread, broken up with fingers
1 tsp salt (5 mL)
Freshly cracked black peppercorns
Vegetable oil for frying

Yogurt Drizzle
1 cup plain whole-fat yogurt (250 g)
½ tsp grated fresh ginger (2 mL)
½ bunch fresh chives or 2 scallions, finely chopped
Sea salt and freshly cracked peppercorns
¼ cup diced grape tomatoes (60 mL)

Coarsely chop the mint and parsley by hand or in a food processor. Transfer to a large bowl with grated onion. Add the cumin, olive oil, egg, Worcestershire sauce, and tomato paste; stir to combine.

Break up the meat and bread with your hands and add it to the onion mixture. Add the seasoning and hand-mix gently until well combined. Cover and chill in the fridge until ready to make patties.

Meanwhile, to make the yogurt drizzle, combine all ingredients in a small bowl and stir together to blend. Adjust the seasoning and chill until ready to use.

To make the meatballs, form the meat-mixture into 12 mounded patties. (Forming into small, mounded patties instead of balls allows for more even cooking.) Add enough vegetable oil to a medium skillet so that it's a 1/2 inch deep; heat over medium high until the oil is hot but not smoking. Fry the meat patties in the oil until evenly browned and cooked through, about 4 minutes per side. Using a slotted spoon, transfer to a paper towel-lined plate.

Serve the still-warm meatballs with minted yogurt and basmati rice.

< MAKES 12 MEATBALLS OR 4 SERVINGS >

GRILLED FLAT IRON STEAK WITH SPICY ONION RELISH

This delicious, low-budget cut—also called a tri-tip—is similar to the flank but doesn't need to marinate. I only cook it on the grill when I want something that's ready in 15 minutes, costs very little, and has phenomenal flavor. This cut has to be served rare or medium rare; if grilled until well done, it will be too tough.

PREP TIME • 10 minutes
COOKING TIME • 10–15 mins
SEASON • summer/fall

Spicy Red Onion Relish

1 Tbsp vegetable oil (15 mL)

2 large red onions, quartered and thinly sliced

2 large sprigs fresh thyme

4 allspice berries

1 small stick cinnamon

½ tsp ground mustard seeds (2 mL)

1 Tbsp brown sugar (15 mL)

1 Tbsp balsamic vinegar (15 mL)

2 Tbsp sherry vinegar (30 mL)

1 dried chili pepper, crushed

1½ lb-piece tri-tip sirloin (750 g)

1 Tbsp olive oil (15 mL)

1 tsp coarsely ground cumin seed (5 mL)

¼ tsp ground cayenne (1 mL)

Sea salt

To make the relish, combine the oil and onions in a medium saucepan over medium heat. Cook, stirring often, until the onions are soft and reduced in size by half, about 6 minutes. Add the thyme, allspice, cinnamon, mustard seeds, brown sugar, balsamic, sherry vinegar, and chili pepper; reduce heat to low and stir well to combine. Cover and cook until the relish is thick, about 17 to 20 minutes. Remove the cinnamon stick and thyme sprigs and set aside until ready to serve. (Cover and refrigerate leftover relish for up to 2 weeks.)

Preheat the grill to high.

Rub the tri-tip with the olive oil, cumin, and cayenne; season with sea salt to taste. Grill for about 7 to 8 minutes per side until an internal temperature of 140°F (60°C) has been reached. Let rest for 5 minutes. Slice the meat thinly across the grain to keep it tender. Serve immediately with relish and your favorite veggies on the side.

< MAKES 4 TO 6 SERVINGS >

BEEF TENDERLOIN WITH WILD MUSHROOMS AND LEEKS

I must have been dreaming of my time in Paris when I wrote this recipe because the mushrooms, cream, and brandy combination is very Parisian. Don't let that rich and slightly decadent mix stop you from making this any day of the week—it's a breeze. And although the sauce sounds rich, it's only a small portion and suits the meat perfectly. In the spring, when in season, use morels: they're spectacular in this dish. Shiitake, chanterelles and king oyster mushrooms also work well.

PREP TIME • 10 minutes
COOKING TIME • 15 minutes
SEASON • spring/fall

Four 2-inch-thick rounds of beef tenderloin (each about 3 oz/75 g)
Sea salt and freshly cracked black peppercorns
2 tsp Worcestershire sauce (10 mL)
1 Tbsp chopped fresh thyme (15 mL)
1 Tbsp grape seed oil (15 mL)
¾ cup chopped wild mushrooms, such as morel or shiitake (175 mL)
2 Tbsp butter (30 mL)
1 small shallot, finely sliced
½ small leek, white part only, cut in half lengthwise and thinly sliced
¼ cup brandy (60 mL)
½ cup beef stock (125 mL)
½ cup 35% cream (125 mL)
Chopped fresh chives, for garnish

Preheat the oven to 350°F (180°C).

Season the beef with salt and pepper, a splash of the Worcestershire sauce and a sprinkling of thyme. In a large skillet over high, heat the grape seed oil until hot. Add the beef tenderloin and sear for about 1 minute per side until just browned.

Transfer to a small roasting pan and roast in the oven for 6 to 8 minutes until medium rare.

Using the same skillet, melt the butter over medium-high heat. Add the mushrooms and sauté until golden, about 2 minutes. Add the shallot and leek and cook for a further 2 minutes until softened.

Deglaze with the brandy. Add the beef stock and cream and continue cooking for 4 to 6 minutes over medium heat until the liquid has reduced and slightly thickened. Adjust the seasoning.

Place the meat on 4 plates. Pour the brandy-cream sauce overtop, garnish with chives, and serve.

< MAKES 4 SERVINGS >

GRILLED STRIP LOIN WITH A MILD HORSERADISH CRÈME FRAÎCHE

The butcher's choice for best steak is the rib-eye but my favorite is the strip loin. Don't get me wrong, I love rib-eye but strip loin has great texture and less fat. The combination of steak and homemade horseradish crème fraîche was a smash at my house when I first served this. I highly recommend the gherkins too: they add a great little crunchy tang.

PREP TIME • 15 minutes
GRILLING TIME • 10–15 mins
SEASON • all seasons

Horseradish Crème Fraîche
>   ¼ cup chilled 35% cream (60 mL)
>   2 small gherkins or small pickles, finely diced
>   2 Tbsp sour cream (30 mL)
>   1 Tbsp freshly grated horseradish (15 mL)
>   1 Tbsp chopped fresh chives (15 mL)
>   Sea salt
>
>   4 AAA or prime strip loin steaks (each about 8 oz/250 g)
>   Olive oil
>   4 fresh sprigs of rosemary, leaves only, chopped
>   Sea salt and freshly cracked black peppercorns

Preheat the grill to high.

To make the Horseradish Crème Fraîche, in a medium bowl, whisk the chilled 35% cream for about 2 minutes or until streaks are visible. Fold in the gherkins, sour cream, and horseradish; season with sea salt. Cover and chill for up to 3 to 4 days in the fridge until ready to use.

Rub the steaks with the olive oil and rosemary and season with salt and pepper. Grill for about 4 to 5 minutes per side for medium rare. If the strip loin steaks are more than 1½ inches thick, reduce the heat to medium high and cook for up to 7 minutes per side. Remove the steaks and let rest on a board for 3 minutes before serving (this prevents the juices from running out all over your plate.)

Serve with the crème fraîche and desired vegetables.

< MAKES 4 SERVING >

PORK AND PEPPER STIR-FRY

I love using a variety of peppers in my stir-fries and salads. The cubanelle is a mild celery-colored green pepper with an oblong shape. It has a very different taste to green bell pepper and one that I prefer. When preparing this, I recommend leaving the pork a little pink in the center to keep it juicy.

PREP TIME • 25 minutes
COOKING TIME • 10 minutes
SEASON • all seasons

2 pork tenderloins (each about 6 oz/175 g)
¼ cup vegetable oil (60 mL)
1 cubanelle pepper, sliced
1 red bell pepper, sliced
1 small onion, sliced
1 celery stalk, sliced
1 small Japanese eggplant, cut in half lengthwise
    and then sliced into ¼-inch semi-circles
1 tsp chopped fresh ginger (5 mL)
1 Tbsp apple butter (15 mL)
¼ cup tamari soy sauce (60 mL)
2 Tbsp hoisin sauce (30 mL)

If serving with steamed rice, start cooking the rice before stir-frying so that both will be ready at the same time.

Slice the pork into ¼-inch-thick medallions. Heat a wok on high and add half the vegetable oil and half the ginger. When the oil is hot but not smoking, add the pork and stir-fry for about 2 minutes until just golden but still soft in the center. Remove the wok from the heat and transfer the pork to a plate; set aside.

Return the wok to high heat and add the remaining oil and the ginger, peppers, onion, celery, and Japanese eggplant. Toss quickly for about 1 to 2 minutes or just until the vegetables begin to soften. If the eggplant absorbs all the oil and is still dry, add ¼ cup of water and cover the wok tightly with a lid. Let the eggplant steam for 2 to 3 minutes until soft.

Remove the lid and toss the vegetables to evenly cook. Add the apple butter, tamari soy sauce, hoisin, and reserved pork. Toss to coat in the sauce and stir-fry for about 1 to 2 minutes or until the pork is cooked but still pink in the center.

Remove and serve with steamed rice immediately.

< MAKES 4 SERVINGS >

GRILLED BUFFALO RIB-EYE WITH SWEET POTATO WEDGES

Buffalo meat is lower in fat and cholesterol than most cuts of beef as well as some cuts of chicken, believe it or not! I was introduced to buffalo, or bison, when I first attended the Calgary Stampede, the world's largest outdoor rodeo, which takes place every year in Alberta. Because buffalo is so much leaner than beef, I like using the rib-eye, which has the most marbling. (You can easily substitute the buffalo for regular beef in this recipe.) I prefer sharing a rib-eye steak because 12 oz is too much for me, which explains why the portions below allow for 4 to 6 servings.

PREP TIME • 10 minutes
COOKING TIME • 15 minutes
SEASON • fall/summer

4 buffalo rib-eye steaks (each about 10 to 12 oz/227 to 284 g)
Sea salt and freshly cracked black peppercorns
2 tsp Worcestershire sauce (10 mL)
Olive oil for rubbing

Sweet Potato Wedges
2 large sweet potatoes, peeled and halved
¼ tsp tandoori seasoning (1 mL)
1 Tbsp vegetable oil (15 mL)
Sea salt

Preheat the grill to high.

Cut each potato half in half, lengthwise, and then cut into 4 wedges; you should end up with 32 wedges in total.

In a medium bowl, toss the wedges with the tandoori seasoning and vegetable oil; season with sea salt.

Transfer to a medium roasting pan or baking sheet and roast for about 13 to 15 minutes, turning occasionally to prevent burning, until the wedges are tender and lightly browned.

Meanwhile, season the buffalo steaks with salt and pepper to taste. Drizzle with a little olive oil and Worcestershire sauce. Grill for about 4 to 5 minutes on each side, for medium rare, or cook until preferred doneness.

Serve the steaks with the sweet potato wedges warm or at room temperature with your favorite salad.

< MAKES 4 TO 6 SERVINGS >

PORK CHOPS WITH MAPLE APPLE JUS

This is a modern interpretation of pork chops and applesauce. The grainy mustard adds crunch and the Granny Smith apple makes it slightly tangy. I had a variety of mouths to feed when I developed this recipe and it was a hit all around. Please cook the pork chops to an internal temperature of 160°F (70°C) (medium well) to avoid the familiar shoe-sole texture of most overcooked chops.

PREP TIME • 10 minutes
COOKING TIME • 20 minutes
SEASON • fall/winter

Four 1½-inch thick loin pork chops,
    bone in (each about 8 oz/250 g)
Sea salt and freshly cracked black peppercorns
2 Tbsp grainy mustard (30 mL)
1 Tbsp olive oil (15 mL)
1 tsp finely chopped fresh thyme (5 mL)
2 sprigs fresh sage, leaves only, chopped
1 Tbsp butter (15 mL)
1 small Granny Smith apple, peeled and diced
    (about ½ inch dice)
2 Tbsp maple syrup (30 mL)
1 tsp tamarind paste (5 mL)
½ cup chicken stock (125 mL)

Preheat the oven to 375°F (190°C).

Season the pork with salt and pepper. Rub with olive oil and chopped thyme and sage and all but 1 tsp of the grainy mustard. Bake for 14 to 16 minutes or until an internal temperature of 160°F (70°C) has been reached.

While the pork is baking, melt the butter in a skillet on medium heat. Add the apple and cook just until golden, about 6 minutes. Add the maple syrup, tamarind paste, and chicken stock; simmer for 2 to 3 minutes or until slightly thickened. Add the remaining teaspoon of grainy mustard and season with salt and pepper to taste.

Remove the chops from the oven and serve with the warm apple-tamarind sauce.

< MAKES 4 SERVINGS >

MISO-CRUSTED RACK OF LAMB WITH A PEAR-BLUEBERRY GLAZE

What kind of a Greek would I be if I didn't give you a lamb recipe?
Mind you, if I served this to my family, they'd say "Miso? What about just
lemon?" This dish requires a little more skill, so I save it for entertaining.
I made this recipe for a James Beard dinner and it was a smash.

PREP TIME • 25 minutes
COOKING TIME • 30 minutes
SEASON • all seasons

2 racks of lamb, Frenched (ask your butcher to do this)
2 cloves garlic, minced
2 Tbsp assorted chopped fresh herbs such as
    thyme and rosemary (30 mL)
½ cup panko (Japanese breadcrumbs) (125 mL)
Kosher salt and freshly cracked black peppercorns
2 tsp white miso paste (10 mL)
2 Tbsp vegetable oil (30 mL)

Pear Blueberry Glaze
    ½ cup unsweetened blueberry juice (125 mL)
    ½ cup pear nectar (125 mL)
    1 Tbsp tamari soy sauce (15 mL)

Preheat the oven to 375°F (190°C).

Trim fat from the lamb, leaving only a thin layer. Score the thin layer of fat in a criss-cross pattern,
being careful not to score the meat underneath. Season the lamb with salt and pepper to taste.

In a small bowl, combine the minced garlic, herbs, and the panko, and toss with your hands
to blend.

Heat the oil in a large sauté pan on medium-high heat. Sear the lamb, bones pointing downwards,
for 1 minute or just until golden. Turn over and sear the other side for 2 to 3 minutes or until
golden. Remove from the pan and cool slightly. Rub the fat side of the lamb with 2 tsp of the
miso paste. Press the herb-panko mixture on all sides of the lamb to completely coat.

Transfer the lamb to a small roasting pan and roast in the oven for 20 to 25 minutes or until
it reaches an internal temperature of 140°F (60°C) for medium rare. Let rest for 5 minutes
before slicing.

Meanwhile, combine the blueberry juice, pear nectar, and tamari soy sauce in a small saucepan
and set over medium heat. Bring to a boil and continue cooking for about 10 to 12 minutes or
until the liquid is reduced and syrupy.

To serve, brush or drizzle a platter with glaze and place the chops on top. Garnish with sprigs
of fresh herbs.

< MAKES 6 SERVINGS >

PROSCIUTTO-WRAPPED INVOLTINI WITH MASCARPONE

These crispy prosciutto-wrapped veal cutlets can be served as a sophisticated appetizer, with a little salad on the side, or as a more substantial main course. The Italian word "involtini" means "a little bundle" and usually involves a filling rolled with some sort of meat wrapping—often veal. The simple sauce—made by deglazing the skillet with Marsala—captures the pure taste of the pan juices.

Four 4 oz veal cutlets, preferably from the leg
Sea salt and freshly cracked black peppercorns
2 Tbsp olive oil (30 mL)
8 very thin slices of prosciutto (about 6 inches long)
Baby arugula, for garnish

Filling
¼ cup good quality mascarpone cheese (60 mL)
2 Tbsp chopped fresh chives (30 mL)
Grated zest of 1 lemon

⅓ cup Marsala (75 mL)

On a cutting board, place the veal cutlets between 2 pieces of plastic wrap and flatten with a mallet until about ⅛-inch thick and 8- x 4-inches long. Cut each in half to create 8 smaller rectangles. Season with salt and pepper to taste.

Heat the oil in a large skillet over medium high until very hot but not smoking. Sear each cutlet for about 30 seconds per side, just until lightly cooked; work with 4 at a time to prevent steaming. Transfer the seared cutlets immediately to a platter, not overlapping, to cool. Remove the pan from the heat.

Meanwhile, combine the mascarpone, chives, and lemon zest in a small bowl until blended. Smear a thin layer of the mascarpone filling overtop the cutlets. Roll one end of each cutlet away from you until it is in the shape of a cigar.

Line up the prosciutto slices in a row on a flat, clean surface. Position each rolled cutlet onto one end of each prosciutto slice; roll until the cutlet is completely wrapped in prosciutto.

Return the skillet to medium heat. Add the prosciutto-wrapped cutlet rolls and cook for about about 2 to 3 minutes, turning often, until crisp on all sides; the pan will be quite browned from the meat drippings. Remove the involtini immediately and deglaze the pan with the Marsala. Decrease the heat to low and keep scraping with a spatula to release the browned bits on the bottom of the pan. Cook for 1 minute more until the sauce is slightly syrupy. Serve 2 involtini per plate, drizzled with the Marsala sauce and garnished with several baby arugula leaves.

< MAKES 4 MAIN COURSE SERVINGS OR 6 TO 8 APPETIZERS >

All I can say is: thank God the low-carb craze is over! I'm always amazed to see what diet craze people believe is the new panacea. The mention of which always brings me back to my stand on balance. I know you've heard it a thousand times, but the best way to enjoy all the delicious food available and to maintain a healthy weight, is to eat a variety of foods, in balance, and to watch the portion sizes.

There are so many varieties of grains and starches that it's virtually impossible to get bored, which keeps cooking fun and full of adventure. I've made some new discoveries myself while creating recipes for this cookbook, like the Klondike Rose potato. Simply using a different variety of potato gave me a whole new flavor experience.

As well, I'll take you down some unusual paths with recipes like Farro Penne, which includes a simple pesto made from pumpkin seeds instead of pine nuts, served over my new favorite wholegrain pasta made from Farro—an ancient Italian grain. This pasta isn't only a nourishing complex carb, it also tastes great.

grains & starches

BEEF BARLEY WITH SMOKED BACON AND CURRANTS

This chewy barley pilaf is my take on a classic beef and barley soup. It makes a great flavorful side starch with the added goodness of the barley. Be sure to purchase the pearl barley, which cooks more quickly. The chunk of deli pork belly bacon will give you a chunkier texture than regular store-bought bacon slices. You can purchase it at your local deli.

PREP TIME • 15 minutes
COOKING TIME • 45 minutes
SEASON • fall/winter

1 Tbsp butter (15 mL)
1 oz smoked bacon, diced (25 g)
1 small onion chopped
1 small carrot, diced
1 clove garlic, chopped
1 cup pearl barley, rinsed and drained (250 mL)
¼ cup dry black currants (60 mL)
3 whole sprigs fresh lemon thyme (or regular)
1 bay leaf
3 cups beef broth (750 mL)
Sea salt and freshly cracked black peppercorns
Several sprigs flat-leaf parsley, chopped

Heat the butter in a large pot over medium. Add the bacon and sauté for 1 to 2 minutes or until golden. Add the onion and carrot and cook for 4 minutes or until softened and golden. Add the garlic and barley and cook for 1 minute.

Add the currants, bay leaf, thyme, broth, and season with sea salt and pepper. Bring to a boil and stir. Cover and simmer on low heat for 35 minutes until tender. Remove from heat and stir in the chopped fresh parsley.

< MAKES 4 TO 6 SERVINGS >

ISRAELI COUSCOUS WITH MINT PESTO

This crunchy couscous is larger than the North African variety and has a chewier texture. I love that it looks like little pearls. By adding the pistachio mint pesto just before serving, you get a burst of fresh mint flavor. It's delicious as a bed under grilled chicken, fish, or lamb.

PREP TIME • 5 minutes
COOKING TIME • 15 minutes
SEASON • all seasons

1 Tbsp olive oil (15 mL)
1 clove garlic, finely chopped
2 cups Isræli couscous (500 mL)
3 cups chicken stock (750 mL)

Pesto

½ bunch fresh mint, thoroughly washed, leaves only
¼ cup fresh shelled pistachios or almonds (60 mL)
¼ cup extra virgin olive oil (60 mL)
Sea salt and freshly cracked black peppercorns

Heat the olive oil in a saucepan over medium low. Add the garlic and cook very gently for about 4 minutes or just until golden. Add the couscous, increase the heat to medium, and stir for about 2 minutes to just slightly toast.

Add the stock, salt, and pepper; bring to a boil. Reduce the heat to low, cover with a tight-fitting lid, and cook for 8 minutes more or until all the liquid is absorbed and the couscous is al dente. Remove from the heat and let stand, covered, for 5 minutes.

Meanwhile, make the pesto by combining the mint leaves with the pistachios in a food processor or by using a large mortar and pestle. Pulse or pound to blend; gradually add the olive oil to achieve a loose paste.

Before serving, fluff the couscous with a fork, add the pesto, and stir.

< MAKES 4 TO 6 SERVINGS >

THAI-FLAVORED FRIED RICE

If I have leftovers after making long grain rice, I make fried rice the next day. You should always start with cold, cooked rice to get the best fried rice results. I also ensure that I'm buying good quality rice that won't fall apart like instant or lower grades. Feel free to add whatever veggies you like or another protein such as chicken, shrimp, or tofu. Thai curry paste is great to keep in the pantry—it's full of flavor and a lot less fuss than trying to make your own. This is a recipe that can be easily halved, if you have less cooked rice on hand.

PREP TIME • 10 minutes
COOKING TIME • 10 minutes
SEASON • all seasons

2 Tbsp vegetable oil (30 mL)
1 to 2 Tbsp Thai red curry paste, or to taste (15 to 30 mL)
3 cups cooked cold long grain rice (750 mL)
¾ cup frozen peas (175 mL)
1 Tbsp ketchup (15 mL)
1 Tbsp tamari soy sauce (15 mL)
2 Tbsp oyster-flavored sauce (30 mL)

Garnish
1 cup bean sprouts (250 mL)
2 green onions, thinly sliced
⅓ cup ground peanuts (75 mL)
Handful of chopped cilantro, optional
Juice of 1 lime

Heat the vegetable oil in a wok or large sauté pan over high heat. Add the Thai curry paste and stir-fry for 1 minute. Add the cooked rice, breaking up the clumps. Continue to stir-fry until heated through, about 2 minutes. If the pan looks dry, add more oil to the stir-fry rice. Add the peas and stir-fry another minute. Add ketchup, tamari soy sauce, and oyster sauce, and cook for 2 more minutes or until the rice is hot throughout.

Garnish with the bean sprouts, green onions, peanuts, and cilantro if using. Squeeze fresh lime juice overtop and serve immediately.

< MAKES 6 SERVINGS >

LIME-SCENTED JASMINE RICE

Jasmine rice is a starchy fragrant rice perfect as a bed for saucy dishes such as stew or stir-fry. Traditionally, jasmine rice isn't cooked with salt— to maintain its distinct fragrance. The addition of kaffir lime leaves gives this dish yet another distinct aroma. Kaffir leaves can be purchased at most specialty Asian stores. I substitute lime zest if I can't find the leaves, although the flavor isn't quite the same.

PREP TIME • 5 minutes
COOKING TIME • 20 minutes
SEASON • all seasons

1 tsp vegetable oil (5 mL)
2 kaffir lime leaves or grated zest of 1 lime
1 cup jasmine rice (250 mL), rinsed in several changes of warm water
1¾ cup water (425 mL)

In a small pot, combine all ingredients and bring to a boil over high heat. Stir, reduce to low, and simmer, covered, for 20 minutes. Remove from heat and let stand 5 minutes before serving.

< MAKES 4 SERVINGS >

KLONDIKE ROSE POTATO WEDGES WITH LEMON MALDON SEA SALT

I've recently discovered this yellow-fleshed red potato variety that is great roasted. (You can substitute any other roasting potato in its place.) Because the salt has rested in the lemon zest for 10 minutes, this simple roast has a unique flavor and aroma. This process draws out the natural oils of the lemon and transfers it to the potatoes. I can taste the difference. Can you?

PREP TIME • 15 minutes
COOKING TIME • 40 minutes
SEASON • all seasons

Finely grated zest of 1 lemon
½ tsp Maldon sea salt or fleur de sel (2 mL)
4 large scrubbed red potatoes, skin on and cut into quarters
3 Tbsp extra virgin olive oil (45 mL)
Cracked black peppercorns

Preheat the oven to 375°F (190°C).

In a small bowl, combine the lemon zest with the salt, stirring to blend. Let stand for 10 minutes.

Meanwhile, in a medium bowl, toss the potatoes with the olive oil. Add the lemon salt to the potatoes and sprinkle with the pepper; toss to combine. Transfer the seasoned potatoes to a large roasting pan and roast, stirring occasionally to prevent scorching, for about 35 to 45 minutes or until the potatoes are golden and crisp.

< MAKES 4 TO 6 SERVINGS >

LINGUINE WITH SCALLOPS, LEMON BROWN BUTTER AND ASPARAGUS

"Ahh, spring"—that's what I remember thinking the first time tasting this dish. All the ingredients are in shades of green and cream and the lemon is quite pronounced. It must be served immediately because the acid in the lemon will turn the veggies a tan yellow color.

PREP TIME • 15 minutes
COOKING TIME • 20 minutes
SEASON • spring

One 1-lb (500-g) pkg linguine
1-lb (500-g) bunch asparagus, trimmed and
    cut into 2-inch (5-cm) pieces
12 large scallops
½ cup green peas, fresh or frozen (125 mL)
⅓ cup butter (75 mL)
Grated zest and juice of 1 lemon
Sea salt and freshly cracked black peppercorns
Handful of fresh parsley, chopped

Bring a big pot of salted water to a boil.

While the water is boiling, melt the butter over medium heat in a 12-inch (30-cm) skillet. Add the scallops and swirl the pan for about 2 minutes to cook while the butter browns. Turn the scallops over and continue to cook the other side for a minute or more, until golden. Transfer the scallops to a plate and set aside. The butter in the skillet should be golden brown but not burnt. Remove the pan from the heat. Add the lemon juice and zest. Remove from heat and set aside.

Add the linguine to the boiling water and cook for 7 minutes or until not quite tender. Add the asparagus pieces and peas to the water and continue boiling for a further 1 to 2 minutes or until the pasta is done al dente (firm to the bite). Drain the pasta, asparagus, and peas, reserving a splash of pasta water. Transfer the drained pasta and vegetables to the pan with brown butter—along with the splash of pasta water—and return to medium heat. Add the scallops and toss to coat. Season with salt and pepper to taste. Transfer to a pasta bowl, sprinkle with chopped fresh parsley, and serve.

< MAKES 4 SERVINGS >

CAVATELLI WITH CHORIZO AND RAPINI

This is the way I like to use cream in my pasta: I add some chicken stock and vermouth to balance the sweet, thick consistency of the cream—this way, I still get the body but it isn't too rich or fatty. The chorizo, a spicy sausage available in Latin American or specialty butcher shops, gives the dish a hot kick. Cavatelli is a shell-shaped pasta with rolled-in edges, but penne will do if you don't have cavatelli.

PREP TIME • 15 minutes
COOKING TIME • 15 minutes
SEASON • fall/winter

One 1-lb (500-g) pkg cavatelli pasta or penne

2 Tbsp olive oil (30 mL)

2 raw spicy chorizo sausages, casing removed, crumbled

1 small onion, chopped

2 cloves garlic, chopped

1 bunch rapini, washed, roughly chopped, and
    blanched in boiling water for 2 minutes

¼ cup vermouth (60 mL)

2 cups grape tomatoes, halved (500 mL)

Handful fresh parsley

¼ cup freshly grated Parmesan cheese, or to taste (60 mL)

½ cup 35% cream (125 mL)

1 cup chicken stock (250 mL)

Bring a large pot of salted water to boil.

Meanwhile, heat the olive oil in a large skillet over medium heat. Add the sausage and cook until golden brown, about 3 to 4 minutes. Add the onion and sauté for 3 minutes or until soft. Add the garlic and sauté for about 1 minute or until softened. Pour in the vermouth to deglaze the skillet before adding the chicken stock. Continue cooking for about 7 minutes or until the liquid has reduced by half. Add the cream and bring back to a simmer. Add the grape tomatoes, cook for 1 minute just to soften, and then remove from heat.

While the sauce is cooking, place a pasta insert—if you have one—into the pot. Blanch the rapini for 2 minutes in the pot to soften. Pull out the pasta insert, draining the rapini, and reserve the boiling water in the pot. Add the blanched rapini to the sauce and set aside.

Return the water to a boil over high heat. Add the cavatelli to the pot and cook for 6 to 7 minutes or until al dente. Drain the pasta, discarding the water, and return the pasta to the dry pot. Pour over the prepared sauce, add the Parmesan and cook for a further minute over medium heat, just until the pasta absorbs some of the sauce. Garnish with parsley, season the pasta with salt and pepper to taste, and serve immediately.

< MAKES 4 TO 6 SERVINGS >

HAZELNUT TABBOULEH

Bulgur grains are wheat kernels that have been steamed, dried, and crushed. They have a tender, chewy texture and can be ground coarse, medium, or fine. The addition of the toasted hazelnuts gives this dish a unique nutty depth. It keeps very well in the fridge and as the flavors improve, you lose some of the crunch.

PREP TIME • 30 minutes
COOKING TIME • 10 minutes
SEASON • all seasons

½ cup fine or medium bulgur (125 mL) or cracked wheat

1 cup boiling water (250 mL)

Sea salt and freshly cracked black peppercorns

½ cup chopped toasted hazelnuts, skinned (125 mL)

½ small English cucumber, diced

1 clove garlic, minced

2 green onions, finely chopped

½ cup chopped fresh mint (125 mL)

1 cup chopped fresh parsley (250 mL)

1 tsp ground cumin (5 mL)

Juice of 1 lemon (about ¼ cup/60 mL)

¼ cup extra virgin olive oil (60 mL)

Preheat oven to 350°F (180°C).

In a medium, dry saucepan, toast the bulgur over medium-high heat for 5 to 7 minutes, stirring occasionally, until the bulgur is brown and makes popping sounds in the pan. Remove from heat and add water and 1 teaspoon salt to pan. Return to heat and bring to a boil. Turn off the heat. Cover and let the bulgur sit for 10 minutes before transferring to a baking sheet to cool.

Meanwhile, spread the hazelnuts on a baking sheet and toast for 7 to 9 minutes until the skins come off when rubbed with a cloth. Transfer hazelnuts to a colander and rub with a tea towel to remove the skins. Discard skins and chop nuts; reserve.

Chop the cucumbers and combine with the remaining ingredients in a medium bowl. Add the cooled bulgur and adjust seasoning before adding the hazelnuts.

< MAKES 6 SERVINGS >

FARRO PENNE WITH A PUMPKIN SEED PESTO

Farro is an ancient strain of wheat that is sometimes misnamed spelt—they're related but not exactly the same. I had to get that off my chest! It's becoming more popular in Italy these days, where it originated, mainly because French chefs in the '90s started making it fashionable. It can be used like barley, in soup, but it's also ground and made into a whole-grain pasta with a little more texture and a nutty taste. It's the only whole-grain pasta that I really like.

PREP TIME • 15 minutes
COOKING TIME • 10 minutes
SEASON • all seasons

One 1-lb (500-g) pkg farro penne or linguine
Sea salt

Pesto
1 bunch fresh basil
1 large clove garlic, peeled
½ cup extra virgin olive oil (125 mL)
¼ cup shelled and toasted pumpkin seeds (60 mL)
1 dried chili pepper, crushed
Grated zest of 1 lemon
Sea salt and freshly cracked black peppercorns

Grated Parmesan cheese and basil leaves, for garnish

Bring a large pot of salted water to a boil.

While the water is boiling, make pesto. Wash the basil thoroughly in cold water and discard the stems. Place the basil in a food processor with peeled garlic and pulse to chop. With the machine running, gradually add olive oil in a slow stream until smooth. Add the pumpkin seeds, chili pepper, lemon zest, salt, and pepper to taste; pulse a few times to finely chop the pumpkin seeds.

Cook the pasta according to instructions for al dente. Drain and toss immediately with pesto to coat. Transfer to a serving platter, sprinkle with grated Parmesan cheese, garnish with basil leaves, and serve.

Note: Farro pasta is a little more delicate than durum wheat, so avoid excessive stirring.

< MAKES 4 TO 6 SERVINGS >

FARFALLE WITH ZESTY SHRIMP

This is a restaurant-style pasta dish that can be made in 20 minutes or so. If you have some frozen shrimp in the freezer and sun-dried tomatoes in a jar, it's a breeze. A great trick for defrosting shrimp is to immerse the plastic bag in cold water and flip a few times. It will thaw in about 30 to 45 minutes.

PREP TIME • 10 minutes
COOKING TIME • 15 minutes
SEASON • all seasons

1 lb (500 g) peeled and deveined large shrimp,
    about 16 to 20, tails on
One 1-lb (500-g) pkg farfalle pasta or any cut shape
¼ cup extra virgin olive oil (60 mL)
2 cloves garlic, cut in slivers
¾ tsp red pepper flakes, or to taste (4 mL)
¼ cup chopped sun-dried tomatoes in oil, drained (60 mL)
Grated zest of ½ lemon
Juice of ½ lemon
Sea salt and freshly cracked black peppercorns
Fresh chopped parsley

Bring a large pot of salted water to a boil. Add the pasta and cook 7 to 9 minutes until al dente. Drain the pasta, reserving some of the pasta water.

While the pasta is cooking, heat the oil in a large sauté pan over medium. Add the shrimp, pepper flakes, and sun-dried tomatoes. Toss for 2 minutes or until the shrimp is golden. Add the garlic and toss for about 1 to 2 minutes or until it softens but doesn't brown.

Remove from heat and add the lemon zest and juice. Add the drained pasta into the sauté pan with the oil and garlic sauce. For a creamier sauce, add some of the pasta water. Season the pasta with salt and pepper to taste. Toss in the parsley and serve immediately.

< MAKES 6 SERVINGS >

GOOEY BAKED MACARONI AND CHEESE WITH BROCCOLI

It's not every day that I make a creamy macaroni dish, but it's good to throw a little gooey fun into the mix every now and then to keep the cravings from taking over. This is a homey, cheesy sauce that can be made in under 20 minutes. I add the broccoli so, with a salad, it's a complete meal.

PREP TIME • 15 minutes
COOKING TIME • 30 minutes
SEASON • all seasons

⅓ cup butter (75 mL)
⅓ cup + 1 Tbsp all-purpose flour (90 mL)
4 cups whole milk (1 L)
¼ tsp grated nutmeg (1 mL)
Sea salt and freshly cracked black peppercorns
1½ cups grated good quality old cheddar cheese (375 mL)
One 1-lb (500-g) pkg macaroni, rotini, fusilli, shells, or elbows
1 head broccoli, florets only
Grated Parmesan cheese, for broiling

Butter a 10- x 12- x 2-inch-deep baking dish.

Cook the macaroni in boiling salted water according to the package directions.

While the pasta is cooking, in a large saucepan over medium heat, melt the butter. Add the flour and stir with a wooden spoon until a paste forms. Remove from heat and add the cold milk, a little at a time, stirring well between each addition. Return to heat once all the milk is added and mixture is smooth. Use a whisk, if needed, to blend the flour. (If you add the milk too quickly without stirring, you'll get a lumpy sauce.)

Continue stirring over medium heat until the sauce boils and thickens. Add the nutmeg and season with salt and pepper to taste. Remove from heat and add the grated cheddar; stir until the cheese melts.

Preheat the broiler.

Two minutes before the pasta is cooked, add the broccoli florets. Drain the pasta and broccoli and toss into the cheese sauce. Transfer to the prepared baking dish. Grate some cheddar cheese on top, if desired, or use Parmesan. Place under the broiler for about 3 to 5 minutes or until browned and bubbly.

< MAKES 6 SERVINGS >

The notion of eating in season is most important in terms of vegetables. Many of the recipes in this chapter came about as I went through my fridge over the year—through spring, summer, fall, and winter—and combined beautifully colored vegetables, an array of spices and herbs, and a variety of cooking techniques.

These cooking techniques, along with my "Pure" food credo (see page 13) of eating in season, were etched into my brain during my year at cooking school in France. Before that time, I thought I was so food savvy. Not! From the French I learned to respect food, and that a tomato salad is only worth having when fresh tomatoes are in season.

It's also with vegetables that we tend to get in a rut, relying on the familiar standbys we grew up with and know how to cook. This is why I've included recipes and cooking techniques for the not-so-familiar, such as ramps, rapini, and Swiss chard. (Of course, now that I've coaxed my set-in-her-ways Greek mother into buying and cooking exotic vegetables and greens like bok choy, anyone can give it a try.)

As in all the chapters, where applicable, I've noted the peak season for recipes. For tips on what's in season and how to best select it, refer to the first chapter: *A Shopping, Organizing and Produce Companion*.

veggies
&
sides

ZUCCHINI AND OLIVE OIL BISCUITS

These savory little biscuits are great on a picnic or for lunch, breakfast, or brunch. Tender and moist, with a golden exterior, they can be topped with dips, cream cheese, and smoked salmon, or eaten just as is.

PREP TIME • 20 minutes
COOKING TIME • 20 minutes
SEASON • summer/fall

1½ cups unbleached, all-purpose flour (375 mL)

¾ tsp baking powder (4 mL)

½ tsp baking soda (2 mL)

⅓ cup fine semolina (75 mL)

½ tsp sea salt (2 mL)

Freshly cracked black peppercorns

⅔ cup buttermilk (150 mL)

⅓ cup good quality extra virgin olive oil (75 mL)

1 large egg

Grated zest of 1 lemon

2 Tbsp chopped fresh chives (30 mL)

1 cup coarsely grated zucchini, about 1 small (250 mL)

Brush the muffin tin with olive oil or line with paper.

Preheat the oven to 375°F (190°C).

In a medium bowl, sift together the flour, baking powder, and soda. Stir in the semolina, salt, and pepper to taste.

In another medium bowl, whisk together the buttermilk, olive oil, egg, lemon zest, and chopped chives until blended. Stir in the zucchini.

Fold the wet ingredients into the dry until just combined; some flour streaks should still be visible. Evenly divide the batter into the prepared muffin tin.

Bake for 18 to 20 minutes or until golden and a tester, when inserted in the middle, comes out dry.

< MAKES 12 BISCUITS >

CREAMED SPINACH WITH RAMPS

I can't get enough of ramps—delicious little wild leeks—when combined with creamy spinach. Ramps are only available for about a month in late spring and have such a unique flavor that I thought I'd share this quick way to cook them. Once the ramps are out of season, you can substitute with green onions or with the white part of regular leeks.

PREP TIME • 10–15 mins
COOKING TIME • 10 minutes
SEASON • spring

1 bunch fresh spinach, thoroughly washed and stems removed
    or a 10-oz (284-g) bag baby spinach
Sea salt and freshly cracked black peppercorns
1 Tbsp butter (15 mL)
2 small ramps (wild leeks), thoroughly washed and sliced
½ cup 18% cream (125 mL)
⅛ tsp freshly grated nutmeg (0.5 mL)
1 Tbsp fresh chopped dill (15 mL)

Before using, wash the spinach several times to remove all the dirt. If using pre-washed baby spinach, wash once.

In a medium saucepan in 2 inches of salted water, cook the spinach over high heat for 2 minutes or until it just wilts. Transfer immediately to a bowl and squeeze out the excess water. Chop into 1-inch (2.5-cm) pieces.

In a medium skillet, sauté the ramps in butter over medium-high heat for 2 to 3 minutes or just until golden. Add the cooked spinach, the cream, grated nutmeg, and the pepper. Simmer, uncovered, for 2 to 3 minutes or just until thick and reduced slightly. Adjust the seasoning and sprinkle with fresh dill.

< MAKES 4 SERVINGS >

SPICY CHIVE CORNBREAD

Cornbread is usually made in a skillet or mold, but with this recipe, I used muffin tins. It resulted in a crisp outer shell and a tender center studded with a crunch from the medium-ground cornmeal. If you're not a fan of the crunch, just use a fine cornmeal. If you'd like to increase the spice, do so in half-teaspoon increments as it could get really fiery. This one is middle-of-the-road spicy. When testing this recipe, we ate half the batch before lunch. I'm just saying.

PREP TIME • 20 minutes
COOKING TIME • 20 minutes
SEASON • all seasons

⅔ cup melted butter, slightly cooled (150 mL)

1½ cups unbleached all-purpose flour (375 mL)

1½ tsp baking powder

½ tsp baking soda (2 mL)

1 tsp salt (5 mL)

1 cup good quality medium-ground cornmeal (250 mL)

3 Tbsp granulated sugar (45 mL)

2 large eggs, separated

1 cup buttermilk (250 mL)

½ tsp finely chopped Thai or Scotch bonnet chili pepper,
   or dried flakes (2 mL)

2 Tbsp fresh chopped chives (30 mL)

Preheat the oven to 400°F (200°C).

Brush the muffin tin with some melted butter and set aside.

Meanwhile, sift together the flour, baking powder, baking soda, and salt. Stir in the cornmeal and sugar.

In a medium bowl, combine the yolks, buttermilk, chilies, and chives. Pour half the buttermilk mixture into the dry mixture and stir well with a rubber spatula; some flour streaks should still be visible. Add the cooled, melted butter and the remaining buttermilk mixture; stir until well combined.

Whip the egg whites in a medium bowl until soft peaks form; fold into the mixture.

Pour the batter into the prepared muffin tin and bake in the middle rack of the oven for about 17 to 20 minutes until golden brown or when a skewer, inserted in the center, comes out dry.

Cool slightly on a wire rack and serve warm, or cool. (Cornbread freezes well if sealed in a plastic bag.)

< MAKES 12 SERVINGS >

BABY SUNBURST SQUASH WITH FRESH PEAS

These colorful little summer squash look like toy tops. Combined with sweet green peas they make a fresh companion to grilled meat, fish, or chicken. The cooking times are a loose guide — I usually pierce the squash with a small knife to check for doneness.

PREP TIME • 10-20 mins
COOKING TIME • 10 minutes
SEASON • summer

¾ lb (375 g) baby squash or patty pan,
　　trimmed and quartered
1½ cups fresh peas (375 mL)
2 Tbsp butter (30 mL)
Sea salt and freshly cracked black peppercorns
1 tsp chopped fresh marjoram or mint (5 mL)

Boil the squash in a medium pot in salted water. After 3 minutes or when the squash is almost tender but still a little firm, add the peas to the same pot and cook for a further 3 minutes or until both are tender; drain.

In a medium sauté pan, melt the butter over medium heat and add the vegetables and herbs. Toss to coat evenly. Season with pepper and serve.

< MAKES 4 SERVINGS >

CHARRED TOMATO TOASTS WITH BASIL PISTOU

"Pistou" is the French term for a pesto that usually has no pine nuts. These little squares of flat bread make a great and versatile appetizer. The cheese garnish can be goat, feta, or Parmesan. The tomatoes have to be in season for that sweet rich flavor to come through. I often make the tomato mixture in advance and store in the fridge. When ready to use, I bring it to room temperature just before serving with freshly grilled bread.

PREP TIME • 20 minutes
COOKING TIME • 15 minutes
SEASON • summer/fall

6 plum tomatoes

Pistou

½ bunch fresh basil, washed and stems removed

3 sprigs freshflat-leaf parsley

1 clove garlic, peeled

½ cup extra virgin olive oil (125 mL)

Sea salt and freshly cracked black peppercorns

1 large Armenian flatbread, cut into 2-inch (5-cm) squares
and grilled for 1 minute per side

Asiago cheese, for garnish

Heat the grill on high.

Place the whole tomatoes on the grill and cook for about 8 minutes on each side or until a dark color is achieved. Keep the lid down to increase the smoky flavor. Check the tomatoes frequently and turn often if they get too dark. Remove from the grill and cool slightly. Using a sharp knife, trim the ends of the tomatoes, and peel and dice into ¼-inch cubes, reserving the juice. Discard peel. Set aside.

To make pistou, in a food processor combine the basil, parsley, and garlic; pulse several times until the mixture is chopped. Add a little oil and pulse again. Turn the motor on and pour the remaining oil in a steady stream until the mixture is smooth. Transfer to a bowl and season with salt and pepper.

Using a wooden spoon, mix together the pistou and tomatoes until well combined. Spoon the tomato mixture onto the flatbread squares. Using a vegetable peeler, "peel" the asiago to make curls. Garnish the flatbread squares with asiago curls and serve.

< MAKES 6 SERVING >

CORN AND PEPPER SUCCOTASH

I just love saying "succotash." It's a southern combination of corn and lima beans but has many variations. This is a quick, fresh version that shows off the summer's harvest. Use fresh lima beans in pods in summer; it's a bit of work, but well worth it. To reduce prep time, you can always opt for frozen lima beans. I do draw the line there though: the corn has to be fresh.

PREP TIME • 20 minutes
COOKING TIME • 15 minutes
SEASON • summer

2 Tbsp butter (30 mL)
1 small onion, chopped
1 red bell pepper, diced
½ jalapeno chili pepper, seeded and chopped
1 clove garlic, chopped
2 cobs of corn, kernels only
1 cup baby lima beans, fresh or frozen (250 mL)
Sea salt and freshly cracked black peppercorns
1 small plum tomato, chopped
2 Tbsp chopped fresh cilantro (30 mL)

Melt the butter in a large skillet over medium-high heat. Add the onion, bell pepper and jalapeno; sauté for 4 minutes to soften. Add the garlic and sauté for 1 minute or just until golden.

Add the corn kernels, lima beans, and tomato and reduce to medium heat; season and cover. Cook for 7 to 10 minutes or until the corn and lima beans are softened. If the pan is dry before the beans and corn are tender, add a few tablespoons of water. Season with salt and pepper to taste and sprinkle with chopped cilantro before serving.

< MAKES 4 TO 6 SERVINGS >

GREEN BEANS WITH CRUNCHY SHALLOTS AND HAZELNUTS

My bean of choice for this recipe would be a French haricot (the skinny bean) but any firm, crisp bean would be delicious. The whole dish takes a few minutes to prepare but the payback is huge. The crunch from the hazelnuts adds a whole different texture to the beans.

PREP TIME • 10 minutes
COOKING TIME • 7 minutes
SEASON • summer/fall

1 lb green beans, (500 g) trimmed only at stem
2 Tbsp butter (30 mL)
2 shallots, finely sliced
¼ cup chopped, toasted and skinned hazelnuts (60 mL)
Sea salt and freshly cracked black peppercorns

Blanch the beans in boiling salted water for about 2 minutes or until just green and still crisp. Drain and set aside.

In a large skillet over medium heat, melt the butter. Add the shallots and stir until golden, about 3 to 4 minutes. Add the hazelnuts and blanched beans and adjust the seasoning. Toss to coat the beans evenly.

Serve with any of your favorite main dishes.

< MAKES 4 TO 6 SERVINGS >

SPICED ROASTED BUTTERNUT SQUASH

This is a delicious veggie dish that boasts the harvest of fall. If the weather is nice, I love to have this golden side, along with a grilled steak, on the barbecue. I simply bundle it all up in foil and keep an eye on the timing. To save some time, buy the pre-cut, peeled squash.

PREP TIME • 10 minutes
BAKING TIME • 20 minutes
SEASON • fall

½ butternut squash, (about 1 lb/500 g) peeled
    and cut into 1-inch (2.5-cm) cubes
½ tsp ground allspice (2 mL)
Sea salt and freshly cracked black peppercorns
2 Tbsp butter (30 mL)
3 sprigs whole thyme
1 sprig rosemary

Preheat the oven to 375°F (190°C).

In a medium bowl, toss the squash with the allspice, sea salt, and pepper to blend. Spread the squash out on a large baking sheet; don't overlap the pieces. Place the sprigs of thyme and rosemary on top and dot with butter.

Roast in the oven for 20 to 25 minutes, stirring often for even browning, or until the squash is tender and golden. (Times may vary depending on the texture of the squash.)

< MAKES 4 SERVINGS >

PEAR, FENNEL AND SQUASH ROAST

This interesting combination of sweet pears, crunchy fennel, and creamy squash screams of fall. The kitchen even smells of fall after its roasted. This dish is great warm but also works at room temperature.

PREP TIME • 15 minutes
ROASTING TIME • 30 minutes
SEASON • fall

1 bulb fennel, trimmed, cored and cut lengthwise
    into ¼-inch (6-mm) slices
½ butternut squash, peeled and cut
    into ¼-inch-thick (6-mm) slices
1 Tbsp chopped fresh rosemary (15 mL)
1 Tbsp chopped fresh sage (15 mL)
2 Tbsp extra virgin olive oil (30 mL)
3 cloves garlic, peeled and quartered
Sea salt and freshly cracked black peppercorns
2 medium, ripe Bosc pears, peeled, cored, and cut in half

Preheat the oven to 375°F (190°C).

Combine all the ingredients except the pears in a large bowl; toss to blend. Season with salt and pepper to taste. Spread the veggies on a large baking sheet or roasting pan and roast about 20 minutes or until they are slightly tender.

Meanwhile, place the pear halves, cut-side down, on a cutting board and slice crosswise into ¼-inch-thick (6-mm) slices.

Add the pears to the vegetables and continue to roast for about 5 to 10 minutes, stirring and turning the vegetables occasionally, or until all the vegetables are tender and golden brown.

< MAKES 4 TO 6 SERVINGS >

PUMPKIN AND TOMATO TAGINE

PREP TIME • 15 minutes
BAKING TIME • 30 minutes
SEASON • fall/winter

I am known for my North African combinations of mixed vegetables with beans or peas. The word "tagine" basically translates as a "stew," and refers to the mixture as well as the traditional cone-shaped clay vessels the stew is cooked and served in. (Tagine clay pots are sold in most gourmet cookware shops.) The taste of this tagine will make you feel like you should be hitching your camel and spending the night in a tent. Couscous is my recommendation for a perfect accompaniment although any rice will do.

1 cup chicken or vegetable stock or water (250 mL)
1 lb new potatoes, cut into bite-sized pieces (500 g)
1 lb pumpkin, squash or sweet potato,
    cut into bite-sized chunks (500 g)
2 cloves garlic, chopped
½ Tbsp salt (7 mL)
1 tsp ground cumin (5 mL)
1 tsp ground coriander (5 mL)
1 tsp ground cinnamon (5 mL)
½ red finger chili pepper, chopped
¼ cup pomegranate juice (60 mL)
1 Tbsp brown sugar (15 mL)
3 Tbsp olive oil (45 mL)
One 19-oz (540-mL) can chickpeas
2 cups (500 mL) Pure by Christine Cushing Tomato Sauce
    or one 14-oz (398-mL) can tomatoes
Chopped fresh cilantro

Combine all the ingredients except the tomato sauce and cilantro, in a 6- to 7-quart (5.7- to 6.6-L) pot. Bring to a boil and reduce heat to medium low. Cover and simmer for 20 minutes or until the vegetables are almost tender. Stir in the tomato sauce and reduce heat to low. Simmer for a further 10 to 15 minutes, stirring occasionally to prevent sticking.

Just before serving, sprinkle with the chopped cilantro.

< MAKES 6 SERVINGS >

PARSNIP AND BRUSSELS SPROUT ROAST

Let the natural flavor of vegetables do the talking. This is a simple winter vegetable roast with beautiful color and the added crunch of natural almonds.

PREP TIME • 10 minutes
ROASTING TIME • 25 minutes
SEASON • winter

2 cups Brussels sprouts, trimmed and cut in half (500 mL)
4 parsnips, peeled and cut into 1-inch (2.5-cm) chunks
2 Tbsp olive oil (30 mL)
2 fresh sprigs savory or sage
Sea salt and freshly cracked black peppercorns
2 red bell peppers, cut into 1-inch (2.5-cm) chunks
½ cup coarsely chopped whole almonds, skin on (125 mL)

Preheat the oven to 375°F (190°C).

Bring a medium pot of salted water to boil. Add the Brussels sprouts and continue boiling on high for about 3 minutes. With a slotted spoon remove the sprouts to a bowl and set aside.

Meanwhile, in a large roasting pan or baking dish, roast the parsnips in oil with the savory sprigs, and season with salt and pepper. After 20 minutes, or when parsnips are just tender but not browned, add the blanched Brussels sprouts, bell peppers, and almonds. Stir to combine, making sure the sprouts are covered with oil. Continue roasting for 7 to 9 minutes or until the peppers are tender and the parsnips golden brown.

< MAKES 4 SERVINGS >

SAVOY CABBAGE WITH BACON AND RIESLING

Savoy cabbage is the darker, curly leafed variety that has a more delicate texture. This would be a great Oktoberfest recipe to feature with a simple sausage or pork recipe. The Riesling and the apple cider really coax out all the flavors in the cabbage. If you buy a meatier bacon at the deli counter, it will add more texture to the dish.

PREP TIME • 15 minutes
BAKING TIME • 20 minutes
SEASON • fall

½ head savoy cabbage, cored
   and sliced ¼-inch (6-mm) thick
1 Tbsp butter (15 mL)
1 small red onion, sliced
2 oz smoked slab bacon, diced (50 g)
1 sprig whole savory
½ cup Riesling white wine
   or other dry white (125 mL)
¼ cup apple cider (60 mL)
1 cup chicken stock (250 mL)
Sea salt and freshly cracked black peppercorns

Boil the cabbage in a small pot of salted water for 2 to 3 minutes or until just tender; drain and reserve.

Meanwhile, in a large skillet, melt the butter over medium-high heat. Add the red onion and sauté for 2 to 3 minutes or until soft. Add the bacon and savory sprig and cook for 2 minutes or until the bacon is golden.

Add the Riesling, apple cider, stock and reserved cabbage, and season. Reduce to medium and cook, covered, for 5 minutes. Remove the cover, reduce heat to low, and simmer for 5 minutes or until soft and tender and the liquid is reduced by half.

< MAKES 4 TO 6 SERVINGS >

ORANGE AND YELLOW SAUTÉED RAPINI

Rapini is one of those vegetables that I'm so addicted to I want to introduce it to everyone! (If you're Italian, then you already know.) It's related to broccoli but slightly bitter—see Chapter 2 for details. You should probably know that I'm having a little fun with the title and it's the orange and the peppers that make the green rapini "orange and yellow" as well as spicy and bold tasting.

PREP TIME • 10 minutes
ROASTING TIME • 10 minutes
SEASON • fall/winter

1 bunch rapini, cut into 3-inch (8-cm) lengths,
    thick stems discarded
Sea salt
2 Tbsp extra virgin olive oil (30 mL)
Grated zest of 1 orange
2 large garlic cloves, thinly sliced
1 finger chili pepper, thinly sliced into rings
1 yellow bell pepper, cut into strips
1 orange, segmented

In a large saucepan, bring 2 quarts (1.9 L) salted water to a boil. Add the rapini and cook until just tender, about 3 minutes; drain.

In a large skillet, heat the olive oil on medium low. Add the orange zest, garlic, and chili pepper; cook until the garlic is golden, about 3 minutes. (Be careful not to burn the garlic at this stage.) Increase the heat to medium high and add the bell pepper; toss for about 2 minutes just to soften slightly.

Add the rapini and cook over moderately high heat until heated through, about 1 to 2 minutes. Add the orange segments, transfer the rapini to a bowl, and serve.

< MAKES 4 SERVINGS >

RED SWISS CHARD GOAT CHEESE GRATIN

A gratin is a dish topped with either some cheese or a breadcrumb mixture and finished under the broiler. In this simple gratin, I love the color of the red Swiss chard and, more interestingly, how it contrasts with the creamy goat cheese. Chard, which is loaded with vitamins and iron, can be substituted with spinach or broccoli in a pinch.

PREP TIME • 10 minutes
BAKING TIME • 20 minutes
SEASON • summer

1 bunch red or green Swiss chard, trimmed
    and cut into 2-inch (5-cm) chunks
Freshly cracked black peppercorns

Béchamel
    1½ Tbsp butter (22 mL)
    2 Tbsp all-purpose flour (30 mL)
    1½ cups cold whole milk (375 mL)
    Pinch freshly grated nutmeg
    4 oz creamy goat cheese, crumbled (100 g)

Preheat the broiler.

Blanch the Swiss chard in salted boiling water for 2 minutes and drain; season with cracked black peppercorns.

Brush an 8- x 10-inch shallow baking dish with olive oil. Arrange the blanched and seasoned Swiss chard on top in a single layer; set aside.

To make the béchamel, melt the butter in a medium saucepan over medium heat. Add the flour and stir with a wooden spoon to combine. Remove the pan from heat and whisk in the cold milk in a steady stream. Continue to whisk until smooth. Return the pan to medium heat. Stir until the mixture thickens and begins to boil. Season the béchamel with salt, pepper, and nutmeg. Stir in the crumbled goat cheese and remove from heat.

Pour the béchamel sauce overtop the chard, spreading evenly to cover. Broil for about 3 to 5 minutes or until golden and bubbly.

< MAKES 8 SERVINGS >

SAUTÉED CAULIFLOWER WITH BLACK MUSTARD SEEDS

Cauliflower is so delicious and under-used, especially considering that it's readily available year round in most grocery stores. A traditional Indian dish was the inspiration for this recipe: the black mustard seeds give it a wonderful flavor and crunch.

PREP TIME • 15 minutes
ROASTING TIME • 15 minutes
SEASON • all seasons

½ lb new potatoes (250 g), cut into 1-inch (2.5-cm) cubes
2 Tbsp olive oil (30 mL)
1 medium onion, chopped
1 head cauliflower, cut into florets
1 Tbsp black mustard seeds (15 mL)
2 cloves garlic, chopped
Sea salt and freshly cracked black peppercorns
4 green onions, sliced
1 Tbsp chopped fresh cilantro (15 mL)
Juice of ½ lime

Put the potatoes in a small pot and cover with water. Bring to a boil and simmer until the potatoes are still firm but cooked through, about 8 to 10 minutes. Drain and set aside to cool.

Meanwhile, heat 1 Tbsp of the olive oil in a large skillet over medium-high heat. Sauté the onions for about 3 minutes or until soft and golden; remove from the pan and set aside.

Heat the remaining olive oil in the same pan over medium. Add the cauliflower and sauté for 2 minutes. Add the mustard seeds and the garlic and sauté for 1 minute more. Season with salt and pepper and pour in ⅓ cup water; cover and steam for 2 minutes. Add the green onions and potatoes; cover and steam for 1 to 2 minutes more or until the cauliflower is crisp-tender. Remove the lid and add the cilantro and lime juice. Adjust the seasonings and serve.

< MAKES 4 TO 6 SERVINGS >

Throughout my life I've had an interesting relationship with baking. As a teenager, I was determined to figure out how all those beautiful pastries and cakes were made because I certainly couldn't master them. After forcing myself to be more precise about the process, I realized I really did love to bake.

Now I absolutely love spending an entire day baking bread or making a spectacular dessert. However, to bake on a more regular basis, I've come up with some easier techniques and innovative combinations to help me enjoy a sweet finale (which is how I'd describe the desserts in this book) to any dinner.

As with the vegetable chapter, the success of many of these recipes depends on the quality and flavor of the fruit. In other words, cooking in season is key.

fruit & desserts

GRAND MARNIER SABAYON OVER TIPSY STRAWBERRIES

This playful dessert illustrates my in-season philosophy: I only serve it when strawberries are at their peak, in summer, to get the maximum fruity flavor. Once the Grand Marnier hits the berries, they release their juices to make a rich syrup in the bottom of the glass. The cracked black peppercorns add an unexpected twist.

PREP TIME • 15 minutes
COOKING TIME • 10 minutes
SEASON • summer

Juice of ½ lemon
1 pint strawberries, washed, hulled, and quartered
Freshly cracked black peppercorns

Sabayon
4 egg yolks
¼ cup granulated sugar (60 mL)
⅓ cup Grand Marnier (75 mL)
¼ cup off dry white wine (60 mL)
Lemon balm leaves, for garnish

In a medium bowl, combine the strawberries, lemon juice, 1 Tbsp Grand Marnier, and pepper. Cover and refrigerate for up to 3 hours or until ready to serve the sabayon.

Meanwhile, in a large stainless steel bowl, combine the egg yolks, sugar, Grand Marnier, and white wine; whisk to dissolve the sugar. Set the bowl over a pot of simmering water on low heat, ensuring that the bottom of the bowl isn't touching the water. Whisk vigorously in a continuous figure-eight pattern for about 5 to 6 minutes. The mixture is ready when it's light, fluffy, and thick. Divide the strawberries into martini glasses or fruit bowls, top with warm sabayon, garnish with a fresh sprig of lemon balm or mint or lavender, and serve immediately.

< MAKES 4 SERVINGS >

KIWI AND HONEYDEW ICE

Italians call it granita; the French, granité; but either way, it's just an ice. This makes such a refreshing dessert in the summer months. It's easy but takes a bit of time—you need to give it a stir every half hour, over several hours—so it's mostly a weekend project. As you freeze it, frequently stir the mixture to break up the ice crystals so the final texture—when fully frozen—is granular. The seeds of the kiwi give it a surprising texture while the basil leaves bring forth an amazing peppery bite.

PREP TIME • 15 minutes
FREEZING TIME • 3 hours
SEASON • summer

8 ripe kiwis, peeled and ends cored
1 ripe honeydew melon, peeled, seeded, and chopped
(about 2 cups/500 mL chopped)
½ bunch fresh basil leaves
Juice of a half lime
⅔ cup unsweetened apple juice (150 mL)
⅓ cup granulated sugar (75 mL)

In a food processor or blender, purée the melon with the basil leaves and lime juice. You can strain the mixture at this point through a coarse sieve to remove all the basil flecks. Add the kiwis, sugar, and apple juice; pulse until smooth.

Transfer to a shallow pan or baking dish. Place on a flat surface in the freezer for 1 hour or until the mixture begins to freeze. Remove from the freezer and stir well with a fork, breaking up the mixture so that no chunks remain. Return to the freezer for a further ½ hour and repeat the stirring process. Repeat this procedure until the mixture has completely crystallized. Keep frozen until ready to serve. To serve, scoop out into tall, chilled martini glasses, garnish with fresh basil leaves and honey dew melon balls, and serve.

< MAKES 8 SERVINGS >

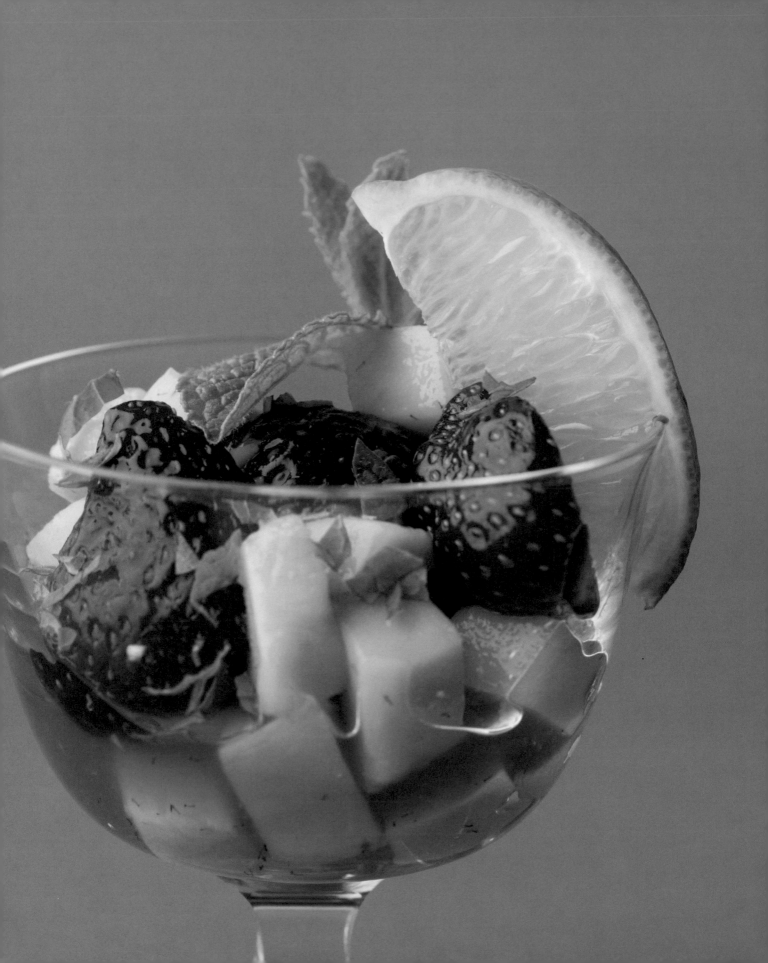

STRAWBERRY MANGO MOJITO SALAD

This refreshing summer dessert combines the delicious lime, rum, and mint combination of a classic Cuban "mojito" with sweet mangoes and ripe strawberries: you won't know whether to serve in it a bowl or glass! Serve over yogurt, ice cream, or completely on its own. You can also go virgin by eliminating the rum.

PREP TIME • 15 minutes
COOKING TIME • none
SEASON • summer

1 pint fresh ripe strawberries, hulled and cut in half
1 medium Atulfo mango, peeled and diced
(Atulfo is less stringy than other varieties)
¼ cup granulated sugar (60 mL)
½ bunch fresh mint leaves, washed and chopped finely
Grated zest and juice of 1 lime,
2 oz white rum (50 mL) or to taste

Combine the strawberries and mango in a medium bowl. Sprinkle with sugar, mint leaves, lime juice, zest, and rum.

Let stand for about 30 minutes to develop its flavor.

For maximum impact, serve in a martini or rock glass with fresh mint sprigs and a lime slice on the rim of the glass.

< MAKES 6 SERVINGS >

WILD BLUEBERRY CLAFOUTI

Traditionally made with tart cherries, clafouti is a French dessert that's essentially a giant thick crêpe scooped out of a baking dish right at the table. This is an ideal summer dessert recipe that can be prepped just before sitting down for dinner. It bakes in 30 minutes, which means it'll be ready by the time you've eaten the main course. Be prepared to share this recipe once you serve it to your guests.

PREP TIME • 10 minutes
BAKING TIME • 35 minutes
SEASON • summer

⅔ cup wild blueberries (150 mL)

1 cup whole milk (250 mL)

½ vanilla bean, seeds scraped

½ cup 35% cream (125 mL)

2 Tbsp sour cream (30 mL)

4 large eggs

½ cup granulated sugar (125 mL)

Grated zest of 1 lemon

3 Tbsp all-purpose flour (45 mL)

Pinch of salt

Butter for baking dish

Preheat the oven to 375°F (190°C).

Butter an 8- x 11-inch oval baking dish. Spread the blueberries on the bottom of the baking dish.

Combine the milk and vanilla bean in a small saucepan over medium-high heat and bring to a boil. Remove immediately from heat. When the milk has cooled slightly but is still warm, add the cream and sour cream; stir well.

To make the custard, whisk together the eggs and sugar until well blended. Whisk in the flour and salt. Continue whisking while gently pouring the milk-and-cream mixture into the egg mixture; blend well.

Pour the custard through a sieve over the blueberries in the baking dish. Sprinkle with grated lemon zest. Bake for 30 to 35 minutes or until the custard is golden and puffed —it will rise and collapse. Let cool just slightly, sprinkle with icing sugar, and serve.

< MAKES 6 SERVINGS >

GOLDEN CUPCAKES WITH POMEGRANATE BUTTERCREAM

There's something about a cupcake that I just can't describe. Even just saying the word "cupcake" makes me feel good. This recipe has been fussed over endlessly to achieve what I think is the ideal delicate texture. They are moist enough to serve without icing, but for you icing lovers, I've included a pomegranate buttercream that takes these cupcakes to new heights.

PREP TIME • 35 minutes
COOKING TIME • 30 minutes
SEASON • winter

⅓ cup + 1 Tbsp softened unsalted butter (90 mL)
⅔ cup granulated sugar (150 mL)
1 Tbsp 35% cream (15 mL)
1 tsp pure vanilla extract (5 mL)
½ cup whole milk (125 mL)
Grated zest of 1 lemon
1 large egg
2 egg yolks
1½ cup cake flour, sifted (375 mL)
2 tsp baking powder (10 mL)
¼ tsp salt (1 mL)

Pomegranate Buttercream
1 cup icing sugar (250 mL)
¼ cup pomegranate juice (60 mL)
½ cup softened unsalted butter (125 mL)

Preheat the oven to 350°F (175°C).

Line a muffin tin with paper liners.

Using a stand mixer with the paddle attachment, beat the butter on medium speed until creamy, about 3 minutes. Add the sugar and continue to beat on medium for about 5 minutes or until light and fluffy. Scrape down the sides of the bowl and beat until smooth. Add the egg, yolks, cream, lemon zest, and vanilla; beat on low speed until blended and smooth.

Sift the flour, salt, and baking powder over a sheet of parchment paper. With the mixer running on low speed, alternate adding the milk and the flour mixture. Lift up 2 sides of the parchment paper to pour in the flour mixture. Beat on medium speed for 1 more minute.

Fill each muffin paper about ¾ full with batter and bake in the bottom third of the oven for about 25 minutes or until a cake tester, inserted into the center, comes out dry.

Cool on wire rack.

To make the icing, in a medium bowl, whip the butter until fluffy, about 3 to 4 minutes. In another small bowl, combine the icing sugar and the pomegranate juice. Whisk until smooth and the sugar is dissolved. Pour slowly into the butter while beating on low speed; continue beating until fully blended. Set aside, tightly covered, at room temperature.

Once the cupcakes are cooled, spread each with the Pomegranate Buttercream and decorate with sparkles or candied violets, or serve as is.

< MAKES 12 CUPCAKES >

QUICK PEAR AND CURRANT CRISP

This is the ultimate "I don't have time to make dessert" dessert and perfect for the drop-in guest. I always have a batch of crisp topping in a sealed container in my freezer ready to layer over fruit. Using the black currant jam as a sweetener in place of sugar and starch gives the fruit layer more texture. I also love this dessert with apples instead of pears. The individual ramekins are a personal touch, but you can easily make it in a square dish.

PREP TIME • 15 minutes
COOKING TIME • 35–40 mins
SEASON • fall

4 ripe Bosc pears, peeled, cored and cut into
    1-inch (2.5-cm) cubes
3 Tbsp black currant jam (45 mL)

Topping
6 Tbsp all-purpose flour (90 mL)
3 Tbsp brown sugar (45 mL)
½ tsp ground cinnamon (2 mL)
Pinch of freshly grated nutmeg
3 Tbsp cold unsalted butter, cut into chunks (45 mL)
⅓ cup rolled oats (75 mL)

Preheat the oven to 350°F (180°C).

In a large bowl, combine the pears and black currant jam; toss to blend.

To make the topping, mix the flour, brown sugar, cinnamon, and nutmeg together. Using the tips of your fingers or a pastry blender, cut the butter into the flour mixture until the mixture resembles coarse meal. Add the rolled oats and stir.

Evenly divide the filling among four 6-oz ramekins. Sprinkle the topping mixture on top of the filling and bake for about 30 minutes or until the top is golden and bubbly.

< MAKES 4 SERVINGS >

SAUTÉED PEARS WITH HAZELNUT PRALINE CREAM

The colors and flavors of fall are reflected in this classic combination of hazelnuts and pears. I was hooked on praline from my year in Paris. And it's so easy to master—if you start with a super clean pot and don't stir the sugar while it's melting, it will behave (sugar is almost as temperamental as chocolate). For a more dramatic twist, use little French pears, whole with stems attached, but cored through the bottom.

PREP TIME • 15 minutes
COOKING TIME • 20 minutes
SEASON • fall

1 Tbsp butter unsalted (15 mL)
2 large Bosc pears, ripe but firm, peeled, and cored
¼ cup red port (60 mL)
1 Tbsp freshly squeezed lemon juice (15 mL)
1 cup cold 35% cream (250 mL)
1 Tbsp icing sugar (15 mL)

Hazelnut Praline
¼ cup hazelnuts, skinned (60 mL)
½ cup granulated sugar (125 mL)

To skin the hazelnuts, toast in a 350°F (180°C) oven for 6 to 8 minutes or until the skins begin to brown. Rub the nuts in a tea towel to remove the skins.

Line a baking sheet with parchment paper.

In a small, heavy-bottomed saucepan on high, heat the sugar until it melts and begins to turn amber. Tilt the pan to prevent any burning spots; be careful as the sugar gets extremely hot. Add the hazelnuts and continue to cook for about 2 minutes or until the sugar turns a rich brown-caramel color. Tilt the pan to blend the sugar; don't stir! Remove from heat immediately and pour onto the lined baking sheet. Let cool completely until hardened. Break up the cooled praline and transfer to a food processor and pulse until the praline is ground to an even texture.

Meanwhile, cut the pears in half lengthwise, and then cut each half into quarters. Sauté the pears in a large skillet over medium-high heat with butter for about 3 to 4 minutes or until the fruit softens and is golden. Add the port and lemon juice; toss for a couple of minutes and continue cooking to just slightly reduce the liquid. Remove from heat.

To serve, whip the cream with icing sugar until peaks begin to form. Fold in the ground praline and serve with the warm sautéed pears. (There will be some hazelnut-praline cream leftover; it keeps for 2 days wrapped in plastic in the fridge.)

< MAKES 4 SERVINGS >

WINTER FRUIT COMPOTE

In the late fall, when the winter months start to creep in, this is a rich, flavorful way to enjoy fruit in their dried form. The addition of cranberries balances the sweetness of the other fruit and makes it perfect for the holiday season. I often make this compote and keep it in my fridge for several weeks as an easy winter drop-in guest dessert. I prefer it with ice cream, yogurt, or a small cake-y thing.

PREP TIME • 10 minutes
COOKING TIME • 30 minutes
SEASON • fall/winter

1½ cups fruity red wine (375 mL)
1 Tbsp balsamic vinegar (15 mL)
2 Tbsp honey (30 mL)
½ cup water (125 mL)
½ vanilla bean, split and seeds scraped
1 cinnamon stick
Several sprigs thyme
1 cup dried apricots (250 mL)
½ cup dried prunes (125 mL)
⅓ cup dried cranberries (75 mL)

In a medium saucepan, combine the wine, vinegar, honey water, vanilla bean (pod and the scraped seeds), cinnamon stick, and thyme sprigs. Bring to a boil over medium-high heat. Cook the mixture for about 10 minutes or until reduced by about one quarter.

Add the fruit, reduce to medium low, and continue to cook, uncovered, for about 20 minutes or until thick and syrupy. Stir the fruit occasionally to prevent scorching. If the liquid level gets too low before the apricots are tender, add a splash more water and keep cooking for a few minutes.

Bring to room temperature and serve over your favorite yogurt, ice cream, or cake. Store the remainder in a well-sealed container in the fridge.

< MAKES 6 SERVINGS >

STICKY TOFFEE THYME BREAD PUDDING

Once you pull this pudding out of the oven, it won't last long. I like eating it still warm, drizzled with the irresistible sticky toffee sauce. The fresh sprigs of thyme give the custard a savory note.

PREP TIME • 10 minutes
COOKING TIME • 35 minutes
SEASON • fall/winter

1 Tbsp unsalted butter (15 mL), for brushing six ½-inch
    (1-cm) thick slices of stale egg bread
3 large eggs
2 cups whole milk (500 mL)
¼ cup granulated sugar (60 mL)
Freshly grated nutmeg
½ vanilla bean, seeds scraped
Pinch salt
¼ cup currants (60 mL)
2 sprigs thyme

Toffee Sauce
1 Tbsp unsalted butter (15 mL)
¼ cup packed brown sugar (60 mL)
⅓ cup 35% cream (75 mL)
2 Tbsp brandy (30 mL)

Preheat the oven to 325°F (160°C).

Break up the bread into bite-size pieces. Brush an 8-½ x 11- x 2-inch-deep oval baking dish with melted butter.

Combine the eggs, milk, sugar, and spices in a medium bowl. Whisk to combine and set aside.

Arrange the broken bread pieces in the baking dish and sprinkle with currants and thyme leaves. Pour the egg mixture overtop; press the bread down to submerge in the mixture.

Bake for about 30 to 35 minutes until puffed and golden but the custard is still moist in the center.

While the bread pudding is baking, in a medium skillet, heat the butter on medium until melted. Add the brown sugar and stir for about 3 to 4 minutes or until the sugar is bubbly and smooth. Add the cream and brandy and reduce heat to low. Stir and continue cooking for 4 to 5 minutes or until the mixture is thick and syrupy.

When the pudding is ready and still warm, pour the mixture evenly overtop. Serve warm.

< MAKES 6 SERVINGS >

COCONUT RICE PUDDING

Rice pudding and cinnamon reminds me of being a kid because my dad would always make it and then line the bowls up on the counter to cool before sprinkling each with ground cinnamon. This version is very grown up and irresistible. The addition of the coconut milk gives a slightly tropical feeling and the dried figs add an unexpected crunch. I also reduce the sugar as I want the flavor of the rice to come through (we all eat way too much sugar anyway).

PREP TIME • 5 minutes
COOKING TIME • 45 minutes
SEASON • all seasons

3 cups whole milk (750 mL)
1 cup low-fat coconut milk (250 mL)
⅓ cup granulated sugar (75 mL)
¼ tsp salt (1 mL)
1 cinnamon stick
¼ cup chopped dried figs (60 mL)
1 vanilla bean, split and seeds scraped
2 strips lemon zest (use a vegetable peeler)
⅓ cup Arborio or other short grain rice (75 mL)
Ground cinnamon, for garnish

In a medium saucepan, combine the sugar, milk, coconut milk, cinnamon stick, dried figs, vanilla bean scrapings, salt, and lemon zest. Bring to a boil on high heat, stirring occasionally. (You can discard the vanilla pod or place in bowl of sugar to make vanilla sugar.) Add the rice and reduce heat to low; simmer, covered, for 20 minutes. Remove the lid and continue simmering, stirring occasionally, for a further 20 to 25 minutes or until the rice is very tender and the pudding begins to thicken.

Remove the zest and cinnamon stick. Stir and divide the mixture into 6 small bowls. Cool to room temperature and sprinkle with ground cinnamon before serving.

< MAKES 6 SERVINGS >

SPONGE TOFFEE

Making this carnival favorite at home is like mastering a science experiment. You need a candy thermometer to accurately gauge the temperature, but it's pretty easy. The baking soda reacts with the liquids and heat and bubbles up like it's the star of a sci-fi movie. To ensure success, use a deep pot to give the blob room to creep up the sides. It's really a riot to watch.

PREP TIME • 5 minutes
COOKING TIME • 15+20 mins
SEASON • fall/winter

Vegetable oil, to grease the pan
1¼ cup granulated sugar (300 mL)
⅓ cup corn syrup (75 mL)
3 Tbsp water (45 mL)
1 tsp pure vanilla extract (5 mL)
1 Tbsp baking soda (15 mL)

Liberally grease a 10-inch-round springform pan with vegetable oil and line the bottom of the pan with parchment paper. Line the sides of the pan with enough parchment paper to create a collar that sits 1 to 2 inches (2.5 to 5 cm) above the pan.

In a deep, medium saucepan, add the sugar, corn syrup, water, and vanilla. Over medium-high heat and without stirring, bring the mixture to a boil. Cook for about 10 minutes until the mixture reaches the hard-crack stage (the temperature should read 300°F (150°C) on a candy thermometer). During the cooking process, if there are any sugar crystals on the sides of the pan, brush the sides of the pan with a clean pastry brush dipped in water.

Remove the sugar mixture from the heat. Working quickly, add the baking soda and whisk for about 5 minutes to incorporate into the sugar mixture. Note that the mixture will bubble up when you add the baking soda so be very careful that you don't get scalded by the hot toffee. Immediately pour the hot toffee into the prepared pan. Let cool and set completely before touching. Break into pieces and serve or store at room temperature in an air-tight container.

< MAKES 12 SERVINGS >

SILKY CHOCOLATE PUDDING

This pudding is the perfect weekend treat—it only takes 20 minutes to cook but should chill for about 3 hours for best results. The quality of your chocolate will reflect the final silky factor. I use regular baking chocolate and the results are remarkably chocolatey. The candied ginger adds a very sophisticated touch.

PREP TIME • 15 minutes
BAKING TIME • 20 minutes
SEASON • all seasons

3¼ cups whole milk (800 mL)
1 vanilla bean, split and seeds scraped or
    1 tsp pure vanilla extract (5 mL)
3 egg yolks
⅓ cup granulated sugar (75 mL)
3 Tbsp cornstarch (45 mL)
½ tsp salt (2 mL)
5 oz semi-sweet chocolate, finely chopped (150 g)
Grated zest of 1 orange
1 tsp chopped candied ginger, optional (5 mL)
1 Tbsp unsalted butter (15 mL)
Whipped cream and candied ginger, for garnish

Slowly bring 3 cups milk, the sugar, and the vanilla seeds to a boil in a heavy-bottomed medium saucepan over medium-low heat. (Discard the vanilla pod or place in a sugar bowl to flavor sugar.) If using vanilla extract, add it in the end with the chocolate to prevent evaporation.

In a medium bowl, whisk together the egg yolks, ¼ cup milk, cornstarch, and salt. Add the hot-milk mixture in a slow stream, whisking constantly, and then pour back into pot.

Cook the pudding gently over medium heat, stirring constantly with a wooden spoon for 1 to 2 minutes or until the mixture boils and thickens. Switch to a whisk towards the end of stirring to ensure a smoother cream. Remove from heat and whisk in the chopped chocolate, grated orange zest, candied ginger if using, and butter.

Divide the pudding among six 6-oz ramekins or small bowls and chill for at least 3 hours. Serve the puddings topped with whipped cream and more chopped candied ginger.

< MAKES SIX 6-OZ SERVINGS >

SPICY CHOCOLATE FONDUE

This fondue makes me feel like I'm back in the time of the Aztecs, who added spices to their velvety chocolate mixtures. I always splurge on a good quality chocolate for the best results. To keep the chocolate smooth, each person gets a bowl and can replenish as needed (if everyone is dipping and double-dipping in the chocolate-fondue pot, the juice from the fruit can seize the chocolate).

PREP TIME • 15 minutes
COOKING TIME • 5 minutes
SEASON • all seasons

Chocolate Fondue

> 6 oz good quality dark chocolate, chopped (175 g)
> 1 cup + 2 Tbsp 35% cream (275 mL)
> 1 Tbsp Kahlua (15 mL)
> ¼ tsp ground cloves (1 mL)
> ⅛ tsp cayenne pepper (0.5 mL)

Suggested Fruit

> 1 mango, peeled
> 1 banana, peeled
> ½ cup lichees, peeled (125 mL)
> 1 star fruit, trimmed

Melt the chocolate in a double boiler over very low heat. At the same time, heat the cream in a saucepan over medium heat until the cream just starts to boil. Stir the cream into the melted chocolate until blended and smooth. Add the Kahlua, cloves, and cayenne to the chocolate and stir. Pour the chocolate mixture into the fondue pot and keep warm.

Peel and cut the fruit into cubes, slices, or wedges. Using fondue forks or skewers, dip the fruit in chocolate.

< MAKES 4 TO 6 SERVINGS >

FRESH FIGS IN SPICY RED WINE

I didn't really appreciate the beauty and taste of a fresh fig until I was in my twenties, despite my mother's ongoing nagging. But now, I wait impatiently for this plump, purple fruit, which is only available in the summer and early fall. I'm completely biased on this, but I prefer the Greek variety. The aim of this recipe is to gently poach the figs for a short time, allowing them to keep their shape but to also infuse them with the rich flavor of the wine and honey.

2 cups fruity red wine (500 mL)
2 Tbsp unsweetened blueberry juice (30 mL)
2 Tbsp honey (30 mL)
1 Tbsp freshly squeezed lemon juice (15 mL)
1 cinnamon stick
6 whole cloves
8 medium fresh purple figs, gently rinsed

In a medium saucepan, combine the wine, blueberry nectar, honey, lemon juice, cinnamon, and cloves; bring to a boil over high heat. Reduce to medium and simmer, uncovered, until the liquid is reduced by a third.

Pierce the figs gently with a fork to allow the poaching liquid to penetrate. (Figs should never be peeled.) Place the figs in the simmering liquid and poach over low heat for 10 to 15 minutes or until the figs are plump. The figs don't need to be completely immersed in liquid when poached.

Remove the figs from the liquid. Increase the heat and boil the liquid for about 10 to 14 minutes or until syrupy.

Serve the figs at room temperature, drizzled with reduced syrup over ice cream, Greek-style yogurt, or a simple sponge cake.

< MAKES 4 SERVINGS >

INDOOR S'MORES (see image on p. 153)

This is a campfire favorite, without the campfire — the whole thing is toasted under the broiler (keep your eye on the smoke detectors!), which is why I suggest serving it in the winter. In the summer, just toast them on the barbecue. I've put another little twist on the traditional s'more by adding sliced bananas and a peanut butter dipping sauce.

PREP TIME • 5 minutes
COOKING TIME • 5 minutes
SEASON • winter

8 small wooden skewers
8 large marshmallows
8 graham crackers
1 banana, sliced into thin rounds
Two thin bars of good quality chocolate (each bar about ¼ lb/125 g)
    cut into 1-inch squares (2.5-cm)

Sauce
¼ cup smooth peanut butter (60 mL)
¼ cup 35% cream (60 mL)

Preheat the broiler.

Skewer the marshmallows onto the ends of the wooden sticks. Place a banana slice in the center of each cracker. Cover with a square of chocolate and arrange on a baking sheet; set aside.

Working with four at a time, line the skewers, with the marshmallows facing away from you, on a baking sheet. Toast the skewered marshmallows under the broiler on one side for 1 to 2 minutes until evenly toasted but not burnt.

Top each graham cracker with a square of chocolate. Remove the marshmallows from the oven and flip each marshmallow, placing the toasted side onto the chocolate-covered graham squares. The marshmallow should completely cover the chocolate to prevent scorching.

Arrange the graham crackers on the same tray, again with the marshmallows facing away from you, working with four at a time. Toast the second side under the broiler until evenly brown, warm, and gooey. The heat from the marshmallow should melt the chocolate. If not, turn the oven to 250°F (120°C) for 2 to 3 minutes to just melt the chocolate.

While the marshmallows are toasting, in a small bowl, stir together the peanut butter and cream until smooth.

Drizzle the warm, toasted s'mores with peanut butter sauce and serve immediately.

< MAKES 4 SERVINGS >

CLASSIC CHOCOLATE CHIP COOKIES

These need no introduction. For a more chocolatey cookie, use
1 cup of chocolate chunks. The better the quality of chocolate,
the better the cookie!

PREP TIME • 15 minutes
BAKING TIME • 12 minutes
SEASON • all seasons

½ cup unsalted butter, room temperature (125 mL)

½ cup packed brown sugar (125 mL)

¼ cup granulated sugar (60 mL)

1 large egg

1 tsp pure vanilla extract (5 mL)

1¼ cups unbleached all-purpose flour (300 mL)

½ tsp baking soda (2 mL)

⅛ tsp salt (0.5 mL)

½ cup dark chocolate chunks or chips (125 mL)

⅓ cup chopped walnuts (75 mL)

Preheat the oven to 350°F (180 °C).

Line 2 to 3 baking sheets with parchment paper or brush with melted butter.
Sift the flour, salt, and baking soda onto another sheet of parchment paper; set aside.

In the bowl of a stand mixer fitted with the paddle attachment or using an electric hand mixer, cream the butter with both sugars on medium speed until light and fluffy. Scrape down the sides of the bowl to blend. Add the egg and vanilla and continue to beat on medium until combined.

Add the flour mixture until just combined. Add the chocolate chips or chunks and walnuts and blend until well mixed.

Drop the batter, 1 tablespoon (15 mL) at a time and at least 2 inches (5 cm) apart, onto the prepared baking sheets. Bake the cookies on separate racks in the oven, rotating the pans halfway through the baking time to ensure even cooking. Bake for 10 to 12 minutes or until the cookies are just firm and golden.

< MAKES ABOUT 24 COOKIES >

CHEWY OATMEAL CRANBERRY COOKIES

This has become my absolute favorite cookie recipe because it's quite low in fat, not too sweet, and made with plenty of oats. I've had the best results with old-fashioned oats, which have a chunkier texture and better flavor. Quick-cooking oats will work but don't use instant. The dried cranberries add a chewy, tart kick. These are insanely addictive.

PREP TIME • 15 minutes
BAKING TIME • 15 minutes
SEASON • all seasons

¼ cup unsalted butter, at room temperature (60 mL)

½ cup packed moscovado or dark brown sugar (125 mL)

1 tsp pure vanilla extract (5 mL)

¼ cup corn syrup (60 mL)

2 Tbsp apple butter (30 mL)

1 large egg

1 cup unbleached all-purpose flour (250 mL)

¼ tsp salt (1 mL)

¼ tsp ground cinnamon (1 mL)

⅛ tsp allspice (0.5 mL)

½ tsp baking powder (2 mL)

½ tsp baking soda (2 mL)

¼ cup whole milk (60 mL)

1½ cups old-fashioned rolled oats (375 mL)

½ cup dried cranberries (125 mL)

Preheat the oven to 350°F (180°C).

Line 2 baking sheets with parchment paper or brush with melted butter.

In the bowl of a stand mixer fitted with the paddle attachment, or using an electric hand mixer, cream together the butter and brown sugar on medium until light and creamy. Scrape down the sides of the bowl to blend. Add the vanilla, corn syrup, apple butter, and egg; continue to beat on medium until well combined.

Meanwhile, sift the flour, salt, cinnamon, allspice, baking powder, and baking soda over another sheet of parchment paper; set aside.

Switch the mixer speed to low and alternately add the flour mixture and the milk to the creamed butter mixture. Continue mixing until just combined. Add the oats and cranberries and beat to just combine.

Drop the batter, 1 tablespoon (15 mL) at a time and at least 2 inches (5 cm) apart, onto the prepared baking sheets. Bake the cookies—one sheet at a time in the middle of the oven—for 13 to 15 minutes or until golden.

< MAKES 24 COOKIES >

PURE GINGER SNAPS

This is the quintessential, crisp ginger snap cookie. For me, it has the right balance of ginger and spice and all things nice. You'll need 2 baking sheets to make all the cookies unless you bake them in two batches. Although you can use a variety of cookie cutters, I use a simple 2-inch-round cutter. The dough can be frozen once you've cut it into disks, or even after baking.

PREP TIME • 15+40 mins
BAKING TIME • 10–12 mins
SEASON • all seasons

½ cup unsalted butter at room temperature (125 mL)

⅓ cup packed brown sugar (75 mL)

⅓ cup molasses (75 mL)

1¼ tsp baking soda (6 mL)

1 Tbsp water (15 mL)

1½ cups unbleached all-purpose flour (375 mL)

1 tsp ground ginger (5 mL)

⅛ tsp ground allspice (0.5 mL)

¼ tsp ground cinnamon (1 mL)

Pinch of salt

In the bowl of a stand mixer fitted with the paddle attachment, or using an electric hand mixer, cream together the butter and brown sugar on low speed until light and fluffy, about 4 to 5 minutes. Scrape down the sides of the bowl to blend.

Pour the molasses into a liquid measuring cup and add the soda and water; stir to combine. Add the molasses to the creamed butter and beat on low speed until smooth.

Sift the flour, spices, and salt onto a sheet of parchment paper or into a medium bowl. Pour this mixture into the batter and continue beating on low speed until the flour is incorporated and a sticky dough has formed.

Turn the dough onto a sheet of plastic wrap and form into a flat rectangle and wrap to completely cover with plastic. Chill for 40 minutes or until the dough is firm enough to roll.

Preheat the oven to 350°F (180°C) and line 2 baking sheets with parchment paper.

Cut the dough in half. Roll each piece on a well-floured surface to about ⅛-inch (3 mm) thickness. Move the dough gently to prevent sticking. Cut out into desired shapes with cookie cutters and place on the prepared baking sheets; repeat with the remaining dough. Bake the cookies for about 10 to 12 minutes or until firm and golden brown. Cool on wire rack.

< MAKES ABOUT 44 COOKIES >

Bibliography

Davidson, Alan. *The Penguin Companion to Food.* London:

Penguin, 2002.

Herbst, Sharon Tyler. *Food Lover's Companion.* Second Edition.

New York: Barrons, 1995.

McGee, Harold. *On Food and Cooking: The Science and Lore

of the Kitchen.* New York: Scribner, 2004.

Wikipedia. www.wikipedia.org.

Willan, Anne. *Reader's Digest Complete Guide to Cookery.*

London: Dorling Kindersley, 1989.